NEIL YOUNG

"THE CANADIAN YEARS"

NEIL YOUNG

DON'T BE DENIED

JOHN EINARSON

QUARRY PRESS

The publisher acknowledges the financial assistance of
The Canada Council and the Ontario Arts Council.

ISBN 1-55082-044-3

Design by Keith Abraham.
Typeset by Larry Harris.
Printed and bound in Canada by
Tri-Graphic Printing, Ottawa, Ontario.

Published in Canada and the United States of America by
Quarry Press, Inc., P.O. Box 1061, Kingston, Ontario K7L 4Y5.

CONTENTS

PREFACE

Neil Young defined himself and his career during his formative years in Canada. Since then he has been reviving, refining, and recreating those early themes and styles. Neil played in Canada for five years, most of that time in Winnipeg-based bands from 1961-1965, then a handful of engagements in Fort William and Toronto over an eight-month period, serving his musical apprenticeship with rock bands in local community clubs and coffee houses. During these seminal years, Neil's songwriting and guitar playing talents were first nurtured as well as his drive to succeed. When I first interviewed Neil in 1986 for a book called *Shakin' All Over* that I wrote on the 1960s rock scene in Winnipeg, I was struck by his clear recollections of people, places, and events from his Canadian years. Those early years hold many warm memories for him. Further discussions revealed the previously undocumented yet pivotal stage of his career performing in Fort William as well as the true story of the months of frustration he experienced while trying to perform in Toronto. When I asked him why so little mention is ever given to those Canadian years, he replied, "No one ever asked me!"

Neil Young's roots are firmly planted in Canadian soil. He has never failed to acknowledge his bond to Canada. Despite residing in California since 1966, he refuses to relinquish his Canadian citizenship. "I'm still proud to be a Canadian. I still feel that someday I could go back and live in Canada."

This is the story of Neil's formative years in Canada.

A triumphant Neil Young comes home to Canada for the Shakin' All Over concert in Winnipeg, 28 June 1987.

Prior to the Shakin' All Over concert, Neil Young and the Squires (above) reunite at the Blue Note Cafe, 27 June 1987. Left to right — Neil Young (lead), Ken Koblun (bass), Bill Edmundson (drums).

Other Squires (below) join Neil to celebrate at the Paddlewheel Restaurant. Left to right — Terry Crosby, Allan Bates, Ken Smyth, Ken Koblun, Jack Harper.

Neil Young (opposite) arrives at the Blue Note reunion looking for The Squires.

Neil poses with biographer John Einarson (below) while signing souvenir copies of Einarson's book Shakin' All Over: The Winnipeg Sixties Rock Scene.

ONE

THE BLUE NOTE REUNION

When we're jamming in our neighborhood,
The girls are dancing
    and they sure look good.
'Cause we're out there like the very first time.
We're prisoners of rock 'n' roll.

PRISONERS OF ROCK 'N' ROLL, 1987

The Blue Note Cafe in Winnipeg, Manitoba is a favorite after-hours hang out for local musicians and friends who congregate in the tiny Main Street club when their gigs are completed. By staying open until past 3 a.m., the club often plays host to major concert attractions who just want to relax after their Arena or Concert Hall performance. Rod Stewart and his band came to the Blue Note following their show at the Arena. So did David Bowie's band. Axl Rose and Slash from Guns n' Roses once dropped by. Impromptu jam sessions are the regular fare after midnight and anyone can take the stage or sit in. Bowie's band held court for two hours, playing old favorites into the wee hours. The club's reputation has been built on this power to attract rock stars — and on the willingness of management to serve drinks after hours while the bands play on.

On the evening of Saturday, June 27, 1987, a party of middle-aged, conservatively dressed couples entered the club well after midnight. They were in the company of a tall, dark-haired man, approximately the same age as the rest of the party but, with long hair, T-shirt, and a black leather jacket, looking decidedly out of place in their company. The waiter at their table took little notice of their faces. "Just some yuppies," he thought as he approached them. One of the party had a proposition for the waiter. If his friend could be allowed to perform, would the drinks be free? The waiter thought for a moment. For Bowie's band or Rod Stewart, sure, but who are you guys? "I'll have to check with the boss," was his reply. Not bothering to look up from his duties at the bar but always eager for a jam session, owner Curtis Riddell nodded his approval. The first round was free, the waiter told the awaiting table, but the second round was half price if he sounded okay.

The long-haired member of the party, the one who was so out of place among the others, strapped on a Telecaster guitar and was joined on the cramped stage by two of the middle-agers, both balding and ponchy, one on drums and the other on bass guitar. Stepping to the microphone the man with the Telecaster announced, "Hi, we're The Squires and this is our first gig in twenty years." And as the group lurched into the old rhythm and blues chestnut, *Baby What You Want Me To Do*, Neil Young and the

Squires were back in 1964 once again. Needless to say, the drinks were free for the next two hours as Neil and his old Winnipeg buddies, those middle-aged rockers with him, relived warm memories of a carefree time when they all shared a dream, to become rock 'n' roll stars.

For Neil Young, that entire weekend was a journey through his past. Over a whirlwind two days, he attended both his old high school reunion and a reunion of his contemporaries on the 1960s Winnipeg music scene. But the highlight was that night at the Blue Note. There, on stage again with Ken Koblun on bass and Bill Edmundson behind the drums, Neil led the band as he had done so long ago, through many songs from their old repertoire. Throughout the entire evening, Neil couldn't stop grinning. Hooking a harmonica into a holder around his neck, Neil led the band into *High Heeled Sneakers*. Introducing that old blues tune, he said: "Here's another one that sounds just like the last one." Midway through the number, Neil missed a verse and called out to the table of friends, "Hey, does anyone remember the words?" Bill, obviously rusty on the drums, was having problems keeping up with Neil's enthusiasm. "Hey Bill," shouted Neil back to him, "come on, we've got plenty of other drummers here!" And indeed they had. Among the party were three more ex-Squires drummers along with two drummers from rival 1960s bands. Jack Harper, Ken Smyth, and Terry Crosby had all drummed for Neil's old band. Allan Bates, Neil's rhythm guitarist in The Squires, was at the table, though he declined to join the jam session. Someone in the audience, having by now recognized who was before him on stage, called out for the rock anthem *Down By The River*. "We don't know that one," Neil smirked. "Some other guy did that one."

Some other guy had indeed done that song, Neil Young the rock legend. On stage here was Neil Young, the skinny kid from the Crescentwood neighborhood who took his guitar wherever he went and could play *Farmer John* better than anybody else on the local community club circuit. That was the Neil Young who played the Blue Note that night. Later that same year, inspired by the jam, Neil organized his own ten-piece rhythm and blues group, dubbing them The Blue Notes. "Obviously, that jam at the

Blue Note Cafe had something to do with it," he confesses.

Memories of his early band, The Squires, remain dear to Neil. "The Squires were the first band that I ever got anything happening with," he states. "We were together a long time, even longer than the Buffalo Springfield. We were pretty young and just learning the business and we were pretty naive, but we had a lot of fun back then." There was, however, one thing that distinguished Neil from the other members of The Squires. "They could have made it. I just wanted it more than they did."

Recently, an acquaintance, upon hearing that I was writing this book, asked if I would be revealing any clues to the complex personality that, to fans of his music and career, is Neil Young. She was rather surprised with my response. Neil is a down-to-earth family man. He cares about his wife and children, trying to maintain as normal a lifestyle for them as possible, cherishes friendship and loyalty, possesses a sharp wit, and worries over the problems our world currently faces. He is more often drawn to support the underdog in most situations, as evident from his involvement in Farm-Aid, and has a warm, sincere, soft-spoken nature. His fame as a singer/songwriter/performer with dozens of gold and platinum albums has changed him little from the teenager in Winnipeg who, like hundreds of other kids his age, dreamed of a career as a musician.

As a child, Neil would tell family and friends that all he ever wanted out of life was to own a chicken farm. He really hasn't strayed far from that humble dream. Although his records still sell in the millions and he remains an icon to several generations of rock, folk, and metal fans, Neil Young runs a ranch in northern California. There, he has surrounded himself with the things he loves — tall trees, rolling hills, green grass, horses, cattle, buffalo, and model trains. His only indulgences are a collection of antique cars and his own state-of-the-art recording studio. He is no gentleman farmer, dabbling in land as a shrewd real estate investment. Broken Arrow ranch is a livestock enterprise, with cattle sold to market and buffalo loaned to Hollywood — a buffalo from Broken Arrow Ranch appeared in Kevin Costner's movie *Dances with Wolves*. When Neil purchased the secluded farmland with royalties from the highly lucrative conglomerate Crosby, Stills, Nash & Young, he set about to make the place home. While Stephen Stills bought mansions in England and David Crosby wasted his wealth and health, Neil cleared land, built barns and fences, and herded cattle. Many of the buildings on the ranch were constructed by Neil himself. His well known back problems in the early 1970s came not as the result of any touring accident or the pressures of a musician's life on the road, but from working on the ranch lifting wood beams. When CSNY needed to rehearse for their 1974 world tour, Neil built the band an enormous outdoor stage on his ranch, the roughly hewn timber cut from his land, nailed together by Neil himself.

For Neil, Broken Arrow Ranch has always been his retreat from the rock 'n' roll treadmill, and his home. Roots are important to him. He experienced a somewhat rootless childhood with the breakup of his family and his own transiency throughout his teens. The ranch has been his stability, a source of strength and inspiration for him. There, he can lead the simple life he harkens to in his song *Country Home* on the RAGGED GLORY album:

I guess I need this city life,
Sure has lots of style.
But pretty soon it wears me down,
And I have to think to smile.
Thankful for my country home,
Gives me piece of mind.
Somewhere I can walk alone,
And leave myself behind.

COUNTRY HOME, 1990

Unlike many of us, Neil has been fortunate in his life to have been able to do what he has always enjoyed most, making music. From his early teens, he decided that music was the one thing that gave him the greatest pleasure and satisfaction. For someone who writes songs so prolifically, he is generally a man of few words. He has always articulated himself best through his music. His determination to make music his life was the guiding focus of his early years and he remains true to that dream today. Asked recently why he continues to maintain a hectic writing, recording, and touring schedule when many of his contemporaries have slowed down their pace, his response was, "It's kind of like having a car and not driving it. If you've got it, you might as well use it."

When people set out to analyze Neil's career with its many twists and turns, the obvious conclusion they reach is that he must be an incredibly complex individual, never satisfied, always searching. He remains one of rock music's most enigmatic personalities, ignoring trends, even his own successes, choosing, instead, to chart his own course, exploring new muscial territories at will. He has riled critics and defied fans in his musical journey over the last twenty-five years or so. As he has often stated throughout his career, he would rather travel in the ditch than the middle of the road. The one consistent thing about Neil Young has been his inconsistency. This, however, is not the product of some schizophrenia or lack of direction on Neil's part. Simply put, Neil loves music, all kinds of music, and finds personal satisfaction in a variety of musical forms. He is a restless soul, always impatient to move on to something new, rarely looking back. He does not like to be labeled. From his earliest years in music, he enjoyed listening to and playing rock 'n' roll, rhythm and blues, folk music, and country. His unique musical vision is a product of all those influences, individually and collectively. He is not content to express himself in one idiom of contemporary music. He hates pigeonholes. "I'm tired of people telling me to do this kind of music or that kind of music," he emphasizes. "It's just music." Where David Crosby sang music is love, Neil's credo is, more aptly, music is life.

Contrary to popular opinion, each move Neil makes is calculated, not impulsive, yet unlike much of today's music, it is not calculated for the current marketplace. He is, above all else, creative, expressing himself in a variety of musical styles by choice. Record companies have sued him in the past for his erratic output, but this has not dampened his resolve to chart his own course. The fact that his uniquely personal vision has received such widespread success for so long is merely a bonus, not a goal. He has rarely courted public acceptance for its own sake, content to soldier on, hoping people will appreciate what he creates. Neil remains true to himself. He has never denied himself his own vision.

Throughout his career, Neil has constantly fought to maintain control over his music. He has recorded complete albums only to shelve them. He is fastidious about the presentation of his music, holding up the release of recordings while he reconsidered song selection or order. Unsatisfied with the quality of an early solo album, he offered to buy the entire first pressing from his label in order to keep it off the market. He is a leader, not a follower, and is often too stubborn, or possessive of his craft, to compromise. His relationships with his post Canadian bands — Buffalo Springfield, Crazy Horse, and Crosby, Stills, Nash & Young — have been erratic at best. He is a willing participant when he feels the need to work within a group environment, but he is just as prone to abandon a collective effort in mid-stream if he feels too confined. Quite simply, Neil has always known what he wanted; he has shown little patience for distractions. His persistence and perseverance at carving out a musical career for himself, despite the pessimism of many, set him apart from his early contemporaries. He was never deterred by failure, drawing strength and determination from it to push on in his quest for acceptance for his music. His teenage obsession with music clouded everything else in his life and drove him to leave his family and friends behind in pursuit of his goal. Since his earliest days in bands, he has remained honest, never compromising his integrity or personal vision. This quality was nurtured very early on in his life and remains constant throughout Neil Young's journey to success.

When so many others didn't, Neil always believed in himself.

TWO

DADDY'S LEAVING HOME

When I was a young boy,
My Momma said to me,
Your Daddy's leavin' home today,
Guess he's gone to stay.
We packed up all our bags,
And drove out to Winnipeg.

DON'T BE DENIED, 1973

In late August 1960, Edna "Rassy" Ragland Young arrived in Winnipeg along with her two sons, seventeen-year-old Bob and fourteen-year-old Neil. The three had packed up their little Ford import with as much as they could take with them and had driven from Toronto across the Canadian Shield to Winnipeg, "Gateway to the West." Left behind in Toronto was husband and father Scott Young. Both this arrival in Winnipeg and this leave-taking would influence Neil Young's life and career enormously.

Neil Young was born in Toronto on November 12, 1945, the year World War II ended. His father, Scott Young, was a writer and later went on to become a noted Canadian journalist and broadcaster. The life of a writer was somewhat transient, and the family was uprooted on several occasions during Neil's childhood. In fact, there were few periods of sustained stability. When Neil was four, the family settled in Omemee, Ontario, a quiet rural community near Peterborough, east of Toronto, immortalized in the lyrics "There is a town in North Ontario . . ." from Neil's song *Helpless* on the Crosby, Stills, Nash & Young album DEJA VU. Neil's warmest childhood memories stem from his time spent in Omemee. The serenity of rural life appealed to him then as it does now. At their home, the family was often in the company of Canada's literary giants, such as Robertson Davies, Farley Mowat, and Pierre Berton. His home environment was stimulating, alive with art and conversation. At the local elementary school Neil gained a reputation as a mischief-maker, a trait which surfaces in his relationship with friends throughout his career.

In 1951, a polio epidemic swept across Canada, striking thousands of young children. Neil was afflicted with the life-threatening ailment and immediately hospitalized in Toronto. Although he recovered, he has since experienced some of the post-polio syndrome fatigue that former patients have suffered. Soon after that, the family followed Scott to Toronto where Neil enrolled in Whitney School. Again, their stay was brief, this time purchasing a home in Pickering, outside of Toronto. By now, signs of estrangement between Scott and Rassy were beginning to surface. Scott was away often and the family never settled anywhere long enough to put down solid roots. In Pickering, Neil began his first ranch enterprise, raising chickens at the back of their property. It was here, too, that Neil played his first musical instrument in the form of a plastic ukulele that he asked his parents to buy him. But once again the family had to pull up stakes for Toronto.

By the summer of 1960, the relationship between Neil's parents had come to an end when Scott announced he was leaving Rassy for another woman. Neil and Bob were informed of the separation by their father over dinner at their favorite restaurant. The break up of the marriage between Rassy and Scott was not smooth. The acrimony was bitter and the wounds deep. Chris Wood, one of Rassy's oldest and dearest friends in Winnipeg sums up Rassy's feelings about the break up: "She felt that she had done a good job helping Scott get going in his career and she just felt that once he started to make it, he ditched her. She was a very proud lady, I guess she got that from her Dad who was from the Southern States and very proud. The divorce hurt her pride but she didn't show it." Nola Halter, another friend states: "She never reconciled to their divorce, ever. She remained bitter toward Scott right through to the end of her life. She would say, 'How the Hell is he going to write anything without me to correct his grammar!'" Nola recalls the night in Toronto in 1982 when Neil was inducted into the Canadian Music Juno Awards Hall of Fame. He had invited both sides of his family to attend the event at the Harbour Castle Hotel Banquet Room. However, he was careful to seat Scott and his relations on one side of the hall, and Rassy and hers on the other. After the presentation, Scott, in a moment of parental pride, approached Rassy's table. "Scott came up to her and said, 'After all is said and done, Ras, isn't this wonderful?' It was an olive branch he was extending, and she just turned her back to him."

As is the sad fallout of most family break ups, the children are caught in the middle, torn apart emotionally by the turmoil and physically by the split up of their parents. At the time of the break up, the two boys were not asked to choose whom they wanted to live with. Neil seemed to need his mother more than Bob; after a few brief months in Winnipeg, Bob ended up back in Toronto with Scott, though that too did not last long. Neil stayed in Winnipeg. Rassy was anxious for the two boys to remain close, though the distance and the circumstances made that difficult.

Neil saw little of his father during those years in Winnipeg.

This explains the sparse coverage of that period in Scott's biography of his successful son, *Neil and Me*. He just didn't know Neil then, and Neil didn't know him. But despite the bitterness his mother harbored towards his father, Neil was never hostile towards him. He respected his father, though he was often uncomfortable in his rare presence.

"I think that Neil was very much in accord with his mother's feelings towards his Dad," reflects Nola Halter, "but he never did battle. He never took sides." Close friends say that Neil rarely spoke of his father. "He treated Neil and his Mom pretty shabbily," says one friend who chooses to remain anonymous. "It was tough at times for the two of them." After the publication of Scott's book on Neil, Rassy called it "a lot of garbage. 'Daddy' this and 'Daddy' that."

The relationship that grew between Neil and his mother provides an important key to his determination to pursue a music career. Quite simply, Rassy loved her son. "The relationship between Neil and his mother was very, very loving," offers Halter. "Rassy was tremendously concerned for Neiler's well-being. She always spoke of him with loving affection. She believed in him. She thought that whatever Neiler did was okay. She was the hingepin behind his determination. I don't think Scott had quite the belief in him that Rassy had." And those feelings were reciprocal. "Neil loved her dearly, deeply and with no sense of obligation," states Halter. "I think they were friends more than just mother and son." Indeed, Neil called his mother Rassy and insisted his friends do the same. "Their personalities really blended. She was a very good mother and I think Neil knew how much she cared for him." Halter adds, "Neil is a richer person because he had Rassy for a mother."

For Rassy, the transition to a new life in Winnipeg was relatively smooth. Though emotions over the break up still ran high, she had family and friends in the city for support. Her father Bill Ragland — or "Rags" as he was known — sister Lavinia Hoogstraten, and chums like Chris and Howard Wood Jr. were all close by. Bill Ragland, an American citizen, had moved to Manitoba not long after the turn of the century and raised his family of three daughters — Vinia, Virginia, and Edna. Because of her father's place of birth, Rassy retained membership in the Daughters of the American Revolution. Her father became a well-known and respected figure around the city and the province

Neil's roots on his father's side are also firmly planted in the Manitoba prairie soil. Born in the farming town of Glenboro, southwest of Winnipeg, Scott had been raised in Winnipeg during the Depression. Neil has relatives in Flin Flon, in northern Manitoba, as well. When Neil played in Winnipeg in 1984 with his band The International Harvesters, his Grandma Jean Young, Scott's mother, made the long journey south for the concert.

Rassy knew the city well. She and Scott had resided here early in their marriage when he worked for the *Winnipeg Free Press*, before heading for more glamorous postings with *The Globe and Mail* newspaper and *Maclean's* magazine in Toronto. She was able to slip comfortably into the Winnipeg social scene, joining both the Granite Curling Club and Niakwa Golf and Country Club. She enjoyed curling with the "Granite Ladies" in winter and golfing with friends during the summer. She was a good tennis player as well, often on the courts at the Winnipeg Canoe Club. Like many Winnipeggers, Rassy enjoyed getting out to the cottage on occasion during the summer. In her case the cottage belonged to Howard and Chris Wood at Clearwater Bay on Ontario's Lake of the Woods, bordering Manitoba's Whiteshell District. Years later when an island property came up for sale across from the Wood's cottage, Rassy contacted Neil to suggest he buy. He considered the offer but passed on it due to other commitments that prevented him from coming up to view the location. After she left Winnipeg in the late 1960s to live in New Smyrna Beach, Florida, Rassy came up every summer to the city, often staying with the Woods. Until 1986, she drove the long journey north and back each summer by herself.

"Rassy was her father's boy," muses Chris Wood. Indeed, Rassy loved the things her father did, sports and the outdoors. After her mother died, Rassy looked after Bill. "She was quite a companion for her dad in his later years," recalls Chris Wood. "She would take him out to his fishing and hunting spots. She would go out with the boys, Rags' buddies, and hunt and fish. They would go each spring to Oak Hammock marsh so he could watch the birds return from migration. She was very good to him." She also possessed another of her father's traits: "Rassy could swear like any of the men," chuckles Chris Wood, "but that was okay because we knew where it was coming from." When Neil, Bob, and Rassy first arrived in Winnipeg, they rented apartment #5 in the Gray Apartments, a small, three story block on the southwest corner of Hugo Street and Corydon Avenue in the working class district of Fort Rouge, two blocks south from her father's apartment in the Debary Apartments, 626 Wardlaw Avenue. Bill later came to live with them in a house on Grosvenor until his death. This modest apartment would remain Neil's home for two years.

Rassy Young was an original, a truly unique character. Anyone who ever had the pleasure of meeting her could never forget her. "Rassy was delicious," laughs Nola Halter. "She was absolutely herself and I enjoyed her immensely." Opinionated to the extreme, she was never afraid to pull any punches. Rassy spoke her mind, always. "She said what she said," muses Chris Wood, "and even though some people wouldn't admit it, she was usually right." Possessed with a dry sense of humor, Rassy was the life of any party and her gravely voice and razor tongue stood out in a crowd. "She was so funny, marvelously witty and very zany," recalls Nola Halter. "She had a little blue English car which she drove in the wrong gear, in the wrong speed, in the middle of two lanes," laughs Nola, "swearing her head off at all these other drivers who got in her way. The road was hers. I was near hysteria in frenzy and frustration driving with her. I dearly loved her but I couldn't take driving with her."

Rassy fought many battles on Neil's behalf and stood up for his career in the early days when few had any faith that he would succeed. "She was absolutely hilarious when she phoned me and told me that Neiler had bought a hearse," laughs Nola. "She said in that droll manner she had, 'Well, if that's what the kid wants.'" When Neil did finally achieve success, Rassy preferred to stay in the background. "That was her style," states Nola. "She was very proud of him and pleased with his success." Though possessed with a gruff exterior, Rassy had a heart of gold as she demonstrated often to friends. "She was always a generous, loyal, and loving person," states Chris Wood. "If she liked you, you were her friend forever." Chris still cherishes the handmade bedspread that Rassy knitted for them.

Shortly after her arrival in Winnipeg, Rassy was approached by Stewart MacPherson of the local CJAY TV station to become a regular panelist on a quiz show entitled "Twenty Questions." MacPherson had originated the show's format, a derivative of "What's My Line," while working in television production in England. After returning to Canada, in the late 1950s, he became an executive with the local television station. Here he sought to revive the show for local audiences. The panelists were allowed to ask up to twenty questions to determine the identity of a person or thing. "Is it animal, vegetable, or mineral?" Each week, Rassy Ragland (as she was known publicly), Bill Trebilcoe, and Nola Macdonald (Halter was her married name) asked questions, seeking clues to the identity of the person or thing, guided by MacPherson. The show was nothing spectacular but was popular locally, lasting until the mid-1960s. At the time, Trebilcoe was a columnist for the *Winnipeg Free Press*, contributing the gossipy "Coffee Break" column. Nola owned a bookstore downtown and was well known in the arts community. The three became close friends and socialized together often. Nola believes that it may have been Scott who secured the role for Rassy, interceding on her behalf with his friend MacPherson, though it is doubtful Rassy would have ever admitted that.

The show is warmly recalled but offered little originality, at least not planned anyway. It was during what broadcasters call the "golden age of live television" which left little room for error or accident. Once, a truck driver walked directly across the set during the show. The flustered panelists carried on. Then the intruder walked back across the set, obviously having delivered his package, oblivious to the cameras and crew. Host Stew MacPherson nabbed the man on his return trip and informed him that he was on live television at that very moment. The stunned driver looked at the camera and said, "My old lady's gonna shit when she sees this!"

The weekly television show provided a modest income for Rassy which supplemented alimony payments from Scott. Between her commitments to the show, her active sports schedule, and the company of old friends, Rassy kept busy enough to avoid the pain of her marriage break up.

Neil had fewer distractions. For him, the move to Winnipeg was more difficult. Living in Pickering and Toronto, he had made many friends, and there were the friends he had from his early years in Omemee. When you are fourteen, having to uproot and relocate to a new city and attend a strange new school can seem like the end of the world. Though Neil had done this frequently during his earlier years, following his father around Ontario, it was especially difficult now as a teenager. Also, this may have been the liberated 1960s, but it was still only the first year of that momentous decade, and attitudes in Winnipeg remained firmly rooted in 1940s and 1950s conservatism. In the typical Canadian middle-class community of the time, divorce was still rare. Being the child of a divorced family, raised by a single parent, carried a stigma back then. Neil carried that baggage with him as he began to integrate into the Fort Rouge teen community. Still, he bore his circumstances well.

"Back then," states Nola Halter, "kids had to apologize for being a child of a single parent. But I don't think Neil ever did." Sensitive as he was, Neil was proud of his mother and their relationship. Close friends confirm, however, that Neil rarely spoke of his homelife. When he did, he would reminisce about the times when his family was together living in Ontario. By all accounts, Neil had a happy childhood prior to the marriage breakup, despite the uprooting he experienced, and Rassy did everything she could to ensure that his happiness was maintained after the split. When his father would pass through Winnipeg, he would arrange to meet with his son. Those times were uneasy for Neil. Friends recall being asked by Neil to accompany him to visit his father, either at his hotel or at a restaurant. "We were all intimidated by who his father was and the fact that he didn't live with Neil," states Pam Smith, a girlfriend of Neil's. "We knew his father was a writer and was on TV. Neil asked me to come with him once to see his father at the Royal Alex Hotel." The Royal Alexandra was Winnipeg's finest hotel in the grand old style of the turn of the century when the railway brought an economic boom to the city. Past its prime, the hotel was demolished in the late 1960s. "I didn't go with him, but I think he was looking for support and I let him down. I don't think he wanted to face his father alone."

The community of Winnipeg began as a summer meeting center for the various tribes of Native Peoples who inhabited the Great Plains to the west and the rugged Canadian Shield to the east and north. Each spring, Natives would canoe down the Red and Assiniboine Rivers to where the two converged at what became known as the Forks. For thousands of years this yearly ritual continued, with the Forks area being merely a seasonal settlement. When French and British adventurers arrived on Canadian shores in the 1600s and established the lucrative trade in furs, the Forks became more than a summer community. Fur traders, first French, then British, erected permanent trading posts at the junction of the two rivers to gather the rich, dark beaver furs trapped by the Natives during the long, cold winter months in the bushlands. Another animal indigenous to the region provided even greater bounty, the buffalo. Herds of thousands roamed the plains. An image of a buffalo appears on Province of Manitoba license plates as well as in the coat of arms for the province.

From these simple origins the community of Winnipeg grew. Much of its transient character was shaped even then. Geographically located at the end of the Shield and the start of the Plains, Winnipeg became a transportation center, the gateway to both the west and the east, for French-Canadian fur trading voyageurs and their half-French half-Indian offspring, the Métis, for young families of Selkirk Settlers forced from their farms in the highlands of Scotland to make way for sheep enclosures, for Ontario loyalists, descendants of British Americans who fled the newly created United States, in horse-drawn wagons moving west in search of new land, and later for eastern European immigrant farmers arriving in Winnipeg on their train journey to new farms on the prairies. Winnipeg has a long history of coming and going, arrivals and departures.

Despite the importance of transportation in Winnipeg's heritage, the city is, in many ways, isolated. Enormous distances, by European standards, separate the city from its nearest Canadian urban neighbors, Toronto to the east and Regina to the west. Its isolation in "the heart of the continent," as a local weatherman used to say, fosters a unique identity among Winnipeggers. Much of that identity is drawn from an 'us against them' sentiment Winnipeggers have towards the rest of the country. They love their own and are more reticent to embrace outsiders. In Winnipeg, you earn your success; it is not bestowed easily. Ask any Winnipeg born entertainer or sports celebrity who has achieved fame beyond the city limits what it is like to play to the hometown crowd. Invariably they will tell you that Winnipeggers are a tough crowd to please. You may be a big shot out there, but back home you have to prove it each and every time.

At the age of fourteen, Neil Young arrived in this tough town, enrolling in grade nine at Earl Grey Junior High School, where he soon joined the crowd and found friends who shared his budding passion for pop music. Earl Grey Junior High was located south of Corydon Avenue, the main thoroughfare in Fort Rouge, east of Crescentwood, on the corner of Cockburn and Fleet. The school was only two blocks from Neil's apartment. Named after the fur trading post built by French Canadian explorer Pierre La Verendrye at the junction of the Red and Assiniboine Rivers, the Fort Rouge area remained largely uninhabited until the late nineteenth century. The district became the bastion of the suburban Anglophone middle class after the turn of the century. Winnipeg experienced a housing boom as a result of the rapid industrialization brought on by the arrival of the Canadian Pacific Railway through the city. As the city spread out, new residential areas like Fort Rouge sprang up, serviced by streetcars at first, then thoroughfares. The houses were wood framed, with picket fences and verandas. At one time, Fort Rouge was a comfortable community, but after World War II, the area had declined somewhat as the middle class moved further south into communities like Fort Garry. By the 1960s, Fort Rouge had a more working class character to it.

Like most residential communities throughout the city at the time, Fort Rouge was bustling with kids. Earl Grey Junior High, named in honor of the former Governor-General of Canada who is best remembered for lending his name to Canada's national football trophy, the Grey Cup, was just one of many schools in the community. Neil soon made himself at home in the community, though he soon wore out his welcome at school. His classmates at Earl Grey remember Neil as a unique character, mischievious and fun-loving with a great sense of humor. Sid Rogers, a classmate, recalls Neil's first day in class. "He came into class and everybody knew he was the new kid. He sat down in his seat and then from the back of the class came this strange noise, like electricity arcing, and it was Neil. He could make that neat sound with his hands. So that was his claim to fame, at least for the first week." Sid goes on to add, "He was a free spirit that some of us jock types had a tough time comprehending. He was interesting to the girls because he played guitar and that probably pissed the jocks off even more. We were aware of who his Dad was, so that gave Neil some respect because we had all read his Dad's books."

Neil still enjoys telling the story of how the school toughs, or "hard rocks" as they were labeled then, pushed him around during his first week at Earl Grey:

When we got to Winnipeg
I checked in to school
I wore white bucks on my feet
When I learned the golden rule

The punches came fast and hard
Lying on my back in the schoolyard.

DON'T BE DENIED, 1973

These lines from his autobiographical song *Don't Be Denied* refer to those early days at Earl Grey. After one incident where a bully knocked his books from his desk, Neil went to the front of the class, picked up a large dictionary, and belted the fellow over the head with it. Despite this incident, Neil was well-liked at Earl Grey. "He was a lot of fun in class" adds Sid Rogers. "He would push the teacher enough to be fun but not enough to get kicked out because that was not fun." Neil is also remembered for his "blue tooth" and black felt fedora hat. His left front tooth had been damaged earlier in childhood, killing the nerves, leaving the tooth a darker, bluey-brown color. He had the tooth capped years later. Twenty-five years later Neil adopted a black fedora again when he fronted The Blue Notes.

"It was a very tough school," says Sue Robertson who attended Earl Grey at the same time as Neil. "But Neil was different, and he made quite an impression on the girls. We thought he was pretty cool because he was tall and very outgoing. He had his hair in a brush cut then. He didn't try to be tough like the other boys and that was unusual." "He was no Ricky Nelson or Elvis Presley, but he was sort of good looking," recalls Susan Kelso, a friend and classmate. "He was the first person we had ever met whose parents were divorced and that made him different. But to our surprise he seemed normal. We had such a limited exposure to that kind of thing. Everybody loved hanging around with him because he had a great sense of humor." Susan relates two memorable examples of Neil's mischieviousness at Earl Grey. "Mr. Yarmie was our science teacher, really stodgy, and hooked on cigarettes. He would leave class every morning around eleven for a cigarette. One day, after he had walked out, Neil made a paper airplane that he called his 'whirly-turd special.' We all started making them and throwing them around. Neil threw his toward the door just as Mr. Yarmie walked back in and it hit him in the head. He got a detention for that." She recalls the next incident. Susan had invited Neil to be co-editor with her and Laurelle Hughes on the yearbook committee. "We used to hold yearbook meetings in an upstairs room of the school. Neil was helping with the yearbook and was up there with us one day. The window was open and there were a whole bunch of stuffed birds stored in the room. So Neil leaned out the window, holding one of these birds as if it was attacking him, so that we could take his picture. At that moment, the principal walked in on us and we all got another detention."

Neil and Susan hung out together often, not really dating, but going to parties or the popular hangout, the Pembina Salisbury House restaurant. "Neither Neil nor I wanted a steady relationship, but we enjoyed being around each other. There was a whole group of us that hung out together — Jim Atkin, Shirley Lord, John Daniel, Harold 'Lou' Westdal, Neil and I. We used to go to the Earl Grey Community Club canteen dances almost every Friday." Friends recall that Neil and Susan were close, though there was nothing serious, just companionship. Neil later accompanied Susan to their Earl Grey graduation dance. They drifted apart when they moved on to Senior High.

Neil spent only one year at Earl Grey Junior High, completing Grade Nine there before graduating to Kelvin High School, but it was an important year for him, his transitional year into the neighborhood. He had made many new friends at Earl Grey, like Jim Atkin. Jim was a popular student, good academically, and a classroom president. Like Neil who had survived the polio epidemic in the early 1950s, Jim had suffered a childhood affliction as well, having been stricken with tuberculosis. It left him with a slight limp in one leg. The two remained close after moving on to Kelvin.

Considering that Neil was the new kid, he had been accepted fairly quickly by others, as his position as co-editor of the yearbook attests. His presence can be found throughout that 1960-61 yearbook, from the photograph of him studying Latin, feet perched atop his desk and his textbook upside down, in the candid photos section. Neil even has a short composition featured in the literature section of the yearbook, under the title, "Why I Chew Gum":

Some people like to chew gum. I am one of them. Chewing gum, in my opinion, is something to do when I'm nervous, playing golf, or just doing nothing. This makes me proud. You see, I'm never caught doing nothing. When I might be caught doing nothing, I'm chewing gum. That's why I chew gum.

BY NEIL YOUNG, ROOM 11

His yearbook write-up confirms his role among his peers: "Neil is the 'happy-go-lucky' guy of our room. He's often seen at Earl Grey Canteen on Friday nights. He is active in the instrumental group called the 'Esquires.'" Already Neil was beginning to establish his reputation as a musician. A photograph from his grade nine graduation party offers a revealing glimpse into his future. Seated on a couch in Neil's apartment are Shirley, Lou, Neil, and Susan. While Shirley and Lou smile for the camera, Neil is preoccupied, intently playing guitar as Susan, seated half on his lap, watches him.

Family friends describe Neil back then as a very likeable young man. "Neil was a very sweet boy in school," recalls Nola Halter. "He had a very sweet, charming manner without any effort at all. He was a beautifully mannered young man, gentle, soft-spoken. And he was very thorough in his explanations to his Mom. She was never in the dark about anything Neil did." Others add that Neil was very kind and gentle, sensitive to people's feelings. He would never intentionally hurt anyone and championed the underdog, perhaps because he viewed himself that way. Such feelings would one day inspire his lyrics in songs like *Nowadays Clancy Can't Even Sing* and *I Am a Child*.

SCHOOL LIFE
1960 - 1961

GRADE NINE   EARL GREY JUNIOR HIGH SCHOOL   HOLLAND STUDIO

Upon arriving in Winnipeg, Neil enrolled at Earl Grey Junior High School. He appears in this class photograph three rows over and three rows down.

The following year he enrolled at Kelvin High School with this portrait appearing in the yearbook.

Neil's mother, Edna "Rassy" Ragland Young, starred on the popular TV program Twenty Questions, shown above flanked by co-panelists Nola Macdonald, Bill Trebicoe, and Stewart MacPherson.

Neil and his mother lived in Gray Apartments, Suite 5 (opposite top) from 1960-1962 before moving to their home at 1123 Grosvenor Avenue.

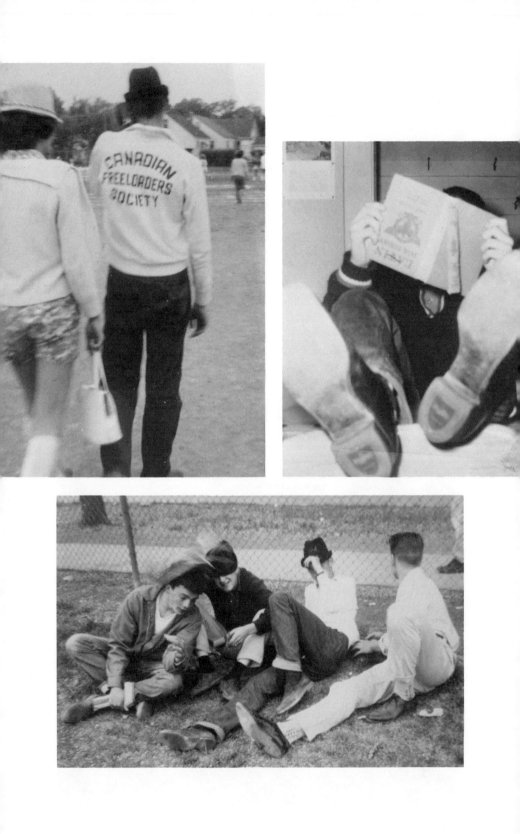

Neil Young of the Canadian Freeloaders Society (opposite) lounges in the school-yard and studies Latin at Earl Grey Junior High.

The portals of Kelvin Technical High (right) closed for Neil when he dropped out of school to become a musician.

YEAR BOOK STAFF

Seated: Jim Atkin, Joann Hagglund, Susan Kelso, Neil Young, Laurelle Hughes, June Hagglund, Ken Koblun. **Standing:** Mrs. Queen, Richard Clayton, Gerry Soucie, Shirley Lord, Mr. Patterson, Ruth Harris, Joe Vinci, Mrs. Mills.

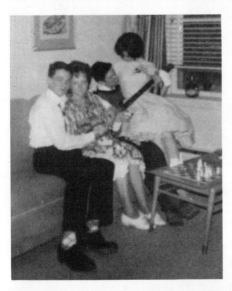

Neil's first published writing appeared in the 1960-61 Earl Grey Junior High Yearbook (above).

Neil appears preoccupied with his guitar in this photo of his Junior High graduation party (left).

The Twilight Zone (opposite top) and the River Heights Community Club (below) were popular teen centers where Neil would perform for enthusiastic audiences.

Neil escorted Jacolyne Nentwig to the River Heights "Humpty Dumpty" Ball in 1962 (below).

One of Neil's early gigs was a fund-raising dance at Kelvin High. In the Kelvin yearbook this photo was entitled "Party" with the caption "Oh Chick, you beautiful thing, don't you ever die."

THREE

DREAMING OF BEING A STAR

Well pretty soon I met a friend
He played guitar
We used to sit on the steps at school
And dream of being stars.

   DON'T BE DENIED, 1973

In Winnipeg, one has to make the most of the long months of winter. For boys, this means playing hockey. As soon as the leaves begin to fall, the sticks and nets, dusty from summer hibernation, emerge from basements or garages throughout the city. Street hockey pacifies them until the outdoor rinks freeze, where you need to be tough enough to endure below zero temperatures in order to play the game. At one stage in the civic history of Winnipeg, the city fathers, in their infinite wisdom, realized that boys have this almost primal urge to play hockey, and sponsored the construction of outdoor rinks in every neighborhood.

To operate those outdoor rinks, the city created community clubs. Ask any Winnipegger, past or present, what community club they attended and watch the warm glow come over them as they speak in reverent tones and misty eyes about Glenwood or Orioles or Crescentwood. These neighborhood clubs were a combined park, recreation center and meeting hall. Each had two or three outdoor rinks, a shack with a wood stove for changing into your skates, and a club house for bingo, community activities, and wedding socials. These socials are a unique Winnipeg tradition. At a social, the prospective bride and groom and their parents host a party for family and friends. Profits from the social are donated to the couple for their start in married life. For Winnipeg teenagers, the thousands of postwar baby-boomers, the community club was *the* place to congregate. "If it hadn't have been for community clubs, a lot of kids like myself would have been juvenile delinquents," states Jim Kale, a contemporary of Neil's from the group Chad Allan and the Reflections. "There were so many activities there for kids. They were the hub of the community."

By 1960, the community clubs were hosting teen dances. At first, these were just record hops organized by enthusiastic parents who acted as hosts and chaperones. An old Caliphone record player would blare out the latest 45 r.p.m.s over the same public address system that the night before had called out bingo numbers. Invariably, the girls sat on one side of the tiny hall and the boys on the other. After a few songs, some of the more outgoing girls would get up and dance with each other, throwing casual glances towards the boys' side. Once that first brave male crossed the floor, the floodgates opened, and before the song had ended, the creaky wood dance floor was full. And it stayed that way all evening. Parent chaperones went around the floor, ever vigilant for young couples dancing too close. Spot dances and lady's choice added to the fun. For a break, kids went to the canteen to buy six cent bottles of Coke, with a straw, of course. At the end of the evening the lights went on, and with parents waiting at the door and the car warming up outside, newly kindled romances were suspended until the following week when it would all start again.

As teen councils came to replace parental volunteers, the dances began to feature live music, but the bands hired were not always your professional outfits with matching suits and slick repertoires. More often these were neighborhood kids, like those in the audience, who had organized a band. The community club dance was the venue for the local guitar players and drummers from your block or high school who found a common love of rock 'n' roll. These were the guys who sat behind you in math class drawing wildly shaped guitars instead of calculating $2xy = 48$ and were the only guys wearing pointed Cuban heel boots, as if they knew something about fashion that the rest of us didn't. They were the guys who claimed to know the real lyrics to *Louie Louie*. Emerging from their basements (it was too cold out there to be a garage band) having mastered the chords to enough songs to make up a set, they would make their world debut on the tiny plywood stage of their local community club. These were the neighborhood celebrities, the guys who knew more than three chords on their Silvertone guitars and could play the lead notes to Duane Eddy's *Rebel Rouser*. By the 1960s, that kind of status earned more attention from the row of bobby socks on one side of the hall than being captain of the hockey team.

This was the kind of celebrity that attracted Neil, and the community clubs interested him not for their hockey rink but their stage. Community clubs offered rock 'n' roll at a grass roots level. "The community club scene was really unique back then," recalls Neil. "There was nothing like it anywhere else. Kids would dance or just watch the band playing. It was a lot of fun." Neil and Jim Atkin acted as MCs for the Friday night canteen dances at Earl Grey Community Club, with Neil as the DJ playing the latest

45s. "Neil and Jim were the big stars at the Earl Grey dances even before Neil played in a band," recalls friend Jacolyne Nentwig. "The girls thought Neil was awesome!"

Stephen Stills, Neil's partner in the Buffalo Springfield and Crosby, Stills, Nash & Young, once said of Neil that he had never played a team sport in his life and could not commit to a band for very long because he just wasn't a team player. He is partially correct. Neil played organized hockey in Pickering before moving to Winnipeg, but once there, true to Stills' observation, Neil did not play any organized sports. He was fourteen, going on fifteen, and had already discovered the guitar. Everything else became secondary to him. Music was going to be his life. Sid Rogers recalls vividly an attempt to coerce Neil into joining the other neighborhood boys in a game of street hockey. "I was at Earl Grey Community Club one day in winter and was trying to get a game of ball hockey going. I saw Neil heading to the club with his guitar. I tried to talk him into coming to play but he insisted that he had to go and practice. So I said to him, 'Neil, give it up, you're never going to make it. You might as well play ball hockey.' Those words still haunt me."

"I knew when I was thirteen or fourteen that that was what I wanted to do," Neil states. "There was nothing else that interested me." In a life that had been turned upside down by the break up of his family, music provided him with a mode of self-expression. Through his guitar, he could express the emotions he felt but couldn't articulate, and later through his own songwriting, Neil could say the things he wanted to say.

Neil had caught the rock 'n' roll bug a few years earlier in Pickering, having witnessed the debut of Elvis on the Ed Sullivan Show. In Toronto, he and a friend would sit on the steps at his school and dream of being Elvis. After a year or two of wrenching chords from his ukulele until his fingers ached, Neil had graduated to a Harmony Monterey model acoustic guitar before coming to Winnipeg. Checking out the bands at the local community club here, Neil made a quick modification to his guitar, adding an electric pick-up to it for amplification. He was now ready for his first group.

That fall, Neil had met John Daniel at school. John, whose parents owned a delivery business in Fort Rouge, Dot Transfer ("Dial

Dot and Dot Dashes"), was a popular student and played guitar. In John, Neil had discovered a kindred spirit. As John remembers, "We were only thirteen or fourteen and Neil and I were in the same classroom. Neil belonged to the Niakwa Golf and Country Club, so I offered to make him a deal. He showed me a little bit of golf and I showed him a few chords on guitar." By then, Neil was an avid golfer with potential. (Neil's brother Bob showed even more promise and later pursued a career in golf.) John Daniel had been playing guitar for awhile and had taken some lessons, but Neil was still just learning the basics on guitar, without the aid of a teacher. John recommended his guitar tutor, Jack Riddell, to Neil, who visited the noted music teacher once or twice. He preferred, however, to teach himself. Neil and John practiced together at their homes before recruiting schoolmates David Gregg on bongo drums and Jim Atkin on vibes, bongo, and conga drums to form a band. Neil chose the name for this, his very first group: The Jades.

Friends recall him making a sign in green lettering spelling out the band's name. The Jades practiced at David Gregg's house and once or twice in Shirley Lord's basement on Garwood Avenue. "My parents' house was one of the few in the area with a rumpus room in the basement and all the kids would hang out there. The band would practice there too." Their repertoire consisted of a few of the more popular guitar instrumentals of the day and the odd vocal song. John played lead guitar and sang, Neil was on rhythm. Their repertoire included numbers by The Ventures and The Fireballs. "We did songs like *Walk, Don't Run, Sorrento*, Pat Boone's *Why Baby* and *I'm Confessin'*. *Fried Eggs* by The Fireballs was our big tune," laughs John.

The Jades played only once, at Earl Grey Community Club. Jim Atkin was president of the Earl Grey Community Club teen council and manager of the band, so he easily secured a booking at the Friday night canteen dance. "We practiced over the Christmas holidays and played our one and only performance after New Year's, 1961, at the Earl Grey canteen dance," recalls David. "All our friends came out to cheer us on." For David and John, it would be their first and last performance. "I slipped on a note in *Perfidia*," John remembers, "and lost my confidence. Neil covered up my slip and no one knew. Even though he was still learning, he was already pretty steady on guitar." That first flush of adrenalin on the tiny Earl Grey Community Club stage fueled a drive in Neil that remains unabated to this day. He has often said that since his first performance he lives to play live.

The Jades soon disbanded. "I had to go to hockey practice when Neil wanted to play guitar," recalls John, "and he told me I had to choose one or the other. I guess I wanted to play hockey." For Neil, music was the priority. Friendship was not enough. Either you were with him all the way or you were out. "There really wasn't anything more important in my life than playing music," states Neil, "and you had to really want to do it and you had to make music first in your life." It would be a pattern that would play itself out many, many times throughout his career.

Each community soon had its own favorite bands and musical xenophobia prevented bands from one community being readily accepted in another. You had to be very good to overcome the fierce territoriality that existed. In the tough North End, bands like The Strollers and The Deverons were kings; Elmwood revered The Galaxies; East Kildonan had Allan's Silvertones; St. Vital had The Jaywalkers; Fort Rouge had Carmine LaRosa and The Thunderstorms. Each contained the best musicians in their community.

By 1963 these regional band identities had begun to blur. The better musicians possessing a more serious outlook — the ones a cut above the 'three chord wonders' — began to seek each other out, regardless of their community roots. Through a process of musical Darwinism, these few select musicians, having progressed through a series of local bands, joined forces. When Allan Kowbel — a.k.a. Chad Allan — of Allan's Silvertones recruited Randy Bachman and Garry Peterson from West Kildonan, and Jim Kale and Bob Ashley from St. Vital, not only did he create the most potent musical unit in the city, he expanded his appeal to two more districts. Randy Bachman, who would later achieve fame with The Guess Who and then with Bachman-Turner Overdrive, was an acknowledged guitar hero already by 1962, and he brought with him to the new group both a high caliber of musicianship and legions of fans who would come to any community club to watch their hero. It was quite a coup for Allan, and the effects reverberated throughout the city. In the North End, The Deverons, led by a cocky fourteen-year-old pianist and singer named Burton Cummings, shed their neighborhood dead weight, bringing in drummer Ron Savoie from St. Boniface and guitarist Bruce Decker from St. James. The addition of both opened up new territories for the group. And so the process went. But the proving ground for beginners remained the local community club.

"If anyone ever asked me when the best times were in music for me," states Fred Turner, later of the multi-platinum Bachman-Turner Overdrive, "it was back in those community clubs. The first gig I ever played was at Orioles Community Club in the west end. We all plugged in to one little amp and no one could hear themselves, so you would have to kick guys in the ankle to get them to change chords. I played for a soft drink and a chocolate bar and I thought I was in heaven." Ron Simenik of The Vaqueros adds, "You played from eight o'clock until one in the morning with a couple of fifteen minute breaks for a few Cokes." And as Neil notes, they played hard, long, and loud — just for the fun of it: "We didn't feel the necessity to stop. All the bands just enjoyed playing there so much and the kids loved it. It was really a fun time. There was always big lineups and always good crowds at the community clubs." Playing hard has always been a Neil Young trait, from these days in the early 1960s to his triumphal recordings and performances with Crazy Horse in the 1970s, 1980s, and 1990s.

It is difficult to pinpoint a particular date or event as a catalyst but around 1963 the Winnipeg music scene virtually exploded throughout the city. Certainly the community clubs were the key ingredient in this thriving music scene, but there were other important factors. The two rival rock 'n' roll radio stations, CKY and CKRC, had discovered the vast, unexploited teen market at these community club dances. Both stations actively promoted community club dances: "Hey there, guys and gals, this is 'PJ the DJ' at KY 58 reminding you to meet me on Saturday night at West End Memorial Community Club along with the fabulous sounds of The Shondels." Imagine, meeting PJ the DJ and hearing The Shondels!

Soon the rock beat throbbed every weekend from the community clubs, church basements, school gymnasiums, even movie theaters on Saturday afternoons. Teen nightclubs sprang up around the city, including The Cellar, The Proteen, The Pink Panther, and The Twilight Zone. Even businesses, witnessing the excitement, sought to tap its potential. Department stores like Eaton's and the Hudson's Bay Company would hire bands to play in their teen fashion departments. Car dealerships had bands playing in their lots. Movie theaters presented bands at Saturday and Sunday afternoon matinees between features. A Champs Kentucky Fried Chicken drive-in restaurant even had a rock group performing on the roof of their building on weekends. The Red River Exhibition, the local fair and circus that still pitches its tents in Winnipeg each June, established its popular Teen Fair, hosting a variety of local bands. There was no shortage of live music for eager teens. By early 1964, there were in excess of two hundred bands gigging around the city, all competing for the same venues. The radio stations began to build their own stable of bands. The Jury and The Deverons worked the CKY-promoted dances accompanied by one of their DJs. The Crescendos and The Quid were favorites of CKRC. The Galaxies went a step further, changing their name to the Club 63 Galaxies after the frequency band number for CKRC. Disc jockeys became celebrities in their own right and could often guarantee a crowd at a dance, regardless of the band. Names like Peter Jackson (PJ the DJ), Doc Steen, Darryl B, Ron Legge, Jim Paulson, and Bob Bradburn were major stars around the city. Television personality Bob Burns carved his own niche in the music scene by hosting Teen Dance Party, an American Bandstand clone every Saturday afternoon on CJAY TV. Besides spinning the latest records, the show featured local bands each week. Burns used his high profile to parlay a major role for himself in management and record production in the city, most notably with Chad Allan and the Reflections, or The Guess Who as they were later named.

It was a truly unique and exhilarating, time and Neil Young was there among it all. "Winnipeg was an exciting place to be growing up in at that time," he states. "It was pretty fruitful back then." As one of the thousands of teenagers who were caught in the whirlwind, he attended community club dances in and around his district. He watched bands performing, learning from the guitar players, absorbing the music and the frenzy they created among the teens. He hung out at the popular teen spots like The Paddlewheel Restaurant on the sixth floor of the downtown Hudson's Bay Store. There, you could see all your favorite local heroes sitting around drinking Cokes and being cool.

With the collapse of The Jades, Neil soldiered on in pursuit of his rock 'n' roll dream. His next step, in the spring of 1961, was a brief stint with an already established Fort Rouge group. The Esquires had earned a name for themselves on the community club circuit and featured a minor celebrity, lead guitarist Larry Wah. Wah had briefly been a member of Allan's Silvertones, which put him a notch above the rest of the pack. He recalls Neil trying out for the band but being unimpressive. "He played rhythm guitar and he was so terrible that we kicked him out after about three practices," laughs Wah. He does remember Neil's determination, marked by a willingness to try another instrument if it meant a place in the band. "We tried switching him to bass but he couldn't even play that." As Neil notes retrospectively, "I was just trying to play rhythm guitar and I didn't know what I was doing." Other members of The Esquires at that time were Gary Reid on guitar, Bob Townsend, bass, Don Marshall, drums, and vocalist Ken Johnson. Jim Atkin was briefly a member of the band during Neil's short tenure.

During his year at Earl Grey Junior High, Neil had also befriended a tall, thin, quiet boy named Ken Koblun, or "Kobie" as he was known to friends then. A long, close friendship soon developed. "I met Neil in my grade nine class and he said he played guitar," recalls Ken, "so I went over to his house to hear him play. I thought to myself 'I can do that too.' I got my dad to buy me a guitar for Christmas and Neil showed me a few things on it." Although Ken was not a member of The Jades, he and Neil struck up a musical relationship soon after the Jades collapsed. Ken would become Neil's most consistent and important partner throughout his musical journey over the next five years. Next to Rassy, no one was closer to Neil than Ken.

Ken Koblun grew up in Fort Rouge and lived with foster families from the time he was a small boy. Perhaps small is an inaccurate description for Ken. By his late teens he stood over six feet, five inches in height. Where Neil was popular, outgoing, and mischievious at Earl Grey, Ken was quiet and withdrawn. Friends recall him as a gentle person who was sometimes picked on for his height and his soft-spoken manner. Ken developed an awareness of music at a young age. "I recall early influences like Les Paul and Mary Ford. When I was twelve I wanted to play the piano but my mother wanted me to play a more transportable instrument like the flute. I didn't settle on the guitar until I was fifteen, after meeting Neil." Ken's first public appearance was on a local TV talent show, backing a neighborhood accordion player. At Neil's request, Ken switched to bass in early 1961. Neil had moved up in instruments as well, after Rassy bought him a second hand Gibson Les Paul Junior electric guitar.

In the fall of 1961, Ken had graduated to Churchill High School in the eastern edge of Fort Rouge. Neil, too, had completed junior high and was enrolled at Kelvin High School in north east River Heights, north of Crescentwood. Neil had already established his reputation as a character by the time he arrived at Kelvin High School. Kelvin was quite a step up from Earl Grey School. Located between old River Heights, bounded to the north by the prosperous Wellington Crescent, and Armstrong Point, the exclusive preserve of Winnipeg's "old money" just across the river from the school, Kelvin had a long and illustrious pedigree. Many of the city's leading figures, including prominent politicians and captains of industry, had attended Kelvin. Its reputation for academic excellence was demonstrated each year as Kelvin teams routinely earned their way into the final rounds of the student quiz show *Reach For The Top*. To attend Kelvin was to be among the elite, socially and economically. By no means a member of that social order, Neil nonetheless numbered among his Kelvin friends Joel Simkin and the Blick brothers, Brian and Barry, all from wealthy Winnipeg families. There was, however, an unstated social barrier at Kelvin. There were the wealthier students from upper-class River Heights and upper-middle-class Crescentwood and those from the more working class Fort Rouge. Although Neil would soon reside in Crescentwood, he had come to Kelvin from Earl Grey in Fort Rouge.

Neil continued to maintain many friends in school. Classmate Susan Cox states, "He was always eccentric. You were never sure how he would react to things." She chuckles as she remembers an incident one warm spring day in 1962. "It was a wonderful day and Neil couldn't stand being inside any longer. When the bell rang, Neil went right out the window and off through the schoolgrounds. Why bother with the door when the window was closer. That was kind of his philosophy." Susan claims to have given Neil his first piano lesson. "We were all selling operetta tickets for a Gilbert and Sullivan production at the school. There was a classroom competition to see which room could sell the most tickets. We all met afterwards at someone's house for hot chocolate and Neil and I sat down at the piano together. I showed him a few notes and he picked it up amazingly fast. He had this wonderful ear and he played in that fashion, so the thought of knowing the notes was totally unnecessary to him."

As a known musician in the school, Neil could always be counted on to play guitar for a fundraising event or pep rally. In April of 1964, Neil and fellow classmate Stuart Adams performed at the Kelvin Charity Week "Cavalcade of Stars" singing three Beatles songs for the student body. Others recall Neil and a French- Canadian student, Gilles Charron, performing songs together in the school cafeteria. Neil's own recollections of his Kelvin schooldays are somewhat dim. He claims his thoughts were more often on music than studies. "I wasn't into school. I really had a pretty good time there," he recalls, "but I really didn't fit in because I wasn't very good in school and I wasn't very interested in being very good in school. I used to spend my time at Kelvin drawing amplifiers and stage setups. I was always flunking out." However, Neil's mischievious nature remained. He is remembered at Kelvin as someone who knew how to have fun. A classmate, Jerry Dykman, recalls Neil sitting at the back of English class singing Roy Orbison's *Pretty Woman*, doing all the growls. The teacher promptly kicked him out.

Although classmates recall his wild sense of humor, those closest to Neil remember another side, a sensitivity that endeared him to the few who were allowed to get really close to him. Two such people were twin sisters Jacolyne and Marilyne Nentwig who attended Kelvin with Neil. Both dated Neil in the early 1960s and became close friends with him. "Neil was a bit insecure about himself," recalls Jacolyne. "His own sense of self-worth wasn't that strong then, partly because of his background, his family split up. He was easily hurt and very sensitive."

Marilyne Nentwig offers an insight into the invisible, yet powerful, social division at Kelvin then. "Who you hung out with was often based on what your parents did and how much money they had. There was a boy that I liked and I thought he was going to ask me to a dance, but he didn't. I found out later through a friend that his parents wouldn't allow him to go out with me because my name was Nentwig, not Smith or something and I lived in Fort Rouge. There was definitely that division and it caused some heartbreak. My sister and I could never join the Humpty Dumpty Club. It was a girls' club from River Heights and they would hold a big ball every year. We used to attend the ball, and Neil escorted Jackie once, but they would never let us join. We were not part of the River Heights crowd. We lived south of that area, 'the wrong side of the tracks' I guess. Neil was and wasn't a part of that crowd. He lived in the area but his family life was such that he was sort of from the other side of the tracks too, so we had that in common."

By this time Neil was gradually drifting way from his Earl Grey friendships. Marilyne adds, "Neil's family situation was tough on him but he never showed it. The normal family then was two parents and he didn't have two, so he felt different." The elite group at Kelvin soon found Neil's celebrity status as a musician an attraction, yet his sense of independence kept him from joining any clique. He had his own identity. As one person states, "Neil was a rebel, but a good rebel."

At the Kelvin High School reunion in 1987, Marilyne and Jacolyne, then eight months pregnant with her sixth child, saw Neil in a crowd but were unable to get close enough to talk with him. Marilyne remarks, "It was strange because all the people who didn't pay much interest in him at school or who used to put him down back then because he didn't fit in, were the one's fawning all over him at the reunion."

The popular hang out for Kelvin students was Stan's Drugstore, on the corner of Stafford and Grosvenor. At the time, the rumor among the teenagers was that Stan's was a bookie joint. Regardless, when not home at noon hour playing guitar, or having lunch at the Wood's house on Kingsway Avenue across from

Kelvin, Neil could often be found at Stan's soda fountain during lunch hour. It wasn't just the beverages that attracted the Kelvin boys to Stan's soda fountain. The girls in their blue tunics from St. Mary's Academy, a Catholic parochial school across the street from Kelvin, frequented Stan's too.

In the fall of 1961, Neil, undaunted by his rejection in The Esquires, had moved on to his next group. The Stardusters, another brief venture, had formed soon after Neil arrived at Kelvin. Little is known about this aggregation, although the band included Neil and Ken Koblun, along with other musicians from Kelvin. Even Neil remains uncertain as to the identity of its members. "I think The Stardusters and The Twilighters were the same group but I can't recall who was in it. There were several names that we used. I remember we had a girl in the band, that was probably Linda Fowler." Rassy adds: "I don't even remember that name. A lot of those bands were the same people but they just changed the band name. Neiler would play with anyone back then." The Stardusters played at a Kelvin dance following an alumni basketball game in February 1962. The yearbook records their appearance: "A dance was held after the game, in River Heights gym, and entertainment was provided by The Stardusters, a Kelvin group that was fabulous! A Mexican Hat Dance and a few Twists broke the ice at the beginning of the dance, and it was pretty hot from then on!"

It was clear to all who knew Neil at Kelvin that school wasn't his priority, as his habit of skipping classes and failing grades proved. His teachers put it down to a lack of motivation more than an absence of ability. The infrequent letters from his father took on a stern tone regarding school. Scott Young had attended Kelvin and he saw Neil as following in his footsteps. There is a unique sociological phenomenon surrounding higher education in the 1960s. Children of the Great Depression in North America, of which Scott Young was one, came out of it with the collective sentiment that the next generation, their children, would never have to suffer what they had endured. Paramount to that resolve was the expectation that their children receive an adequate education, something many of them had to foresake in order to help support the family. This, in large part, accounts for the higher percentage of university graduates in the 1960s than in previous decades. These grads were the offspring of that lost generation from the Depression. As his father saw it, at the very least, Neil would be expected to complete high school, then hopefully go on to university. Much earlier, back in Omemee, Neil had expressed an interest in attending agricultural college. That is how his father viewed the situation from 2200 kilometers away. Here in Winnipeg, however, things were different. There was a side to Neil his father had yet to witness, and when he did learn of Neil Young the musician, he refused to accept it for a long time. Rassy, too, wanted Neil to complete his education, but she was more willing to accept Neil as he was and support his decisions.

Neil's less than serious attitude towards school and his increasing preoccupation with music culminated in his failing grade ten in June, 1962. The news was not taken well by his mother, nor by his father in Toronto. Neil agreed, however, to try again and returned to repeat the grade in the fall of that year. Flunking a grade carried a certain notoriety that only enhanced Neil's reputation as a rebel at Kelvin. Unfortunately, Neil's resolve to work harder in his second try at grade ten did not last long. Once again, music was to come before school.

Around this time, Neil and his mother had moved from their apartment on Hugo and Corydon to the second floor of a stately old home at 1123 Grosvenor Avenue in the more well-heeled Crescentwood district, north of Corydon Avenue. Despite the fact that Rassy only rented a suite there, the house on Grosvenor would remain Neil's permanent address until he moved to Toronto in 1965. Nestled among tall, shady oak trees, the three-story brick and stone house with its side entrance off the sidewalk is what real estate agents today term a "character home." It's size and elegance typified the old established WASP character of the surrounding area, and the house still retains a regal charm despite the years. Neil had his own large bedroom where he would often retreat to play his guitar, write songs, and dream of a career in music. Neil's grandfather, Bill Ragland, eventually moved in with them, occupying the third floor attic room.

Rassy was often away from home, either pursuing one of her sporting activities or working on the television show. Neil learned to fend for himself at an early age, making meals and going his own way. "He wasn't exactly served three square meals a day, like the rest of us," states later bandmate Allan Bates. "Before a gig, Neil would cook us all up macaroni and cheese." Neil's favorite food was Kraft macaroni and cheese dinner, though friends recall he loved canned spaghetti as well. "Not much has changed," remarks Neil's wife Pegi, smiling. Neil had a lot more freedom than his peers, at an early age. This sense of independence would serve him well throughout his life. It allowed him to do whatever was necessary to further his career without being dependent on anyone. Neil owes no one for his success. "I knew what needed to be done to make it and I was willing to make those sacrifices."

With Ken Koblun over at Churchill and Neil at Kelvin, the two had a larger pool of musicians to draw on for their next endeavor. The Classics, formed in the fall of 1962, lasted longer than his previous associations, performing six engagements before disbanding. Consisting of Fort Rouge musicians Buddy Taylor on drums, Jack Gowanlock from Kelvin on rhythm guitar, and piano player Linda Fowler from The Stardusters, along with John Copsey on vocals, Ken on bass guitar, and Neil on lead guitar, The Classics made their debut at Churchill High School on November 17th. Their second engagement was at Kelvin one week later. Playing the hits of the day along with instrumental numbers by Johnny and the Hurricanes, The Ventures, and Duane Eddy, The Classics were anything but classic. They lasted four more gigs, including Morse Place Community Club in East Kildonan and Riverview Community Club in Fort Rouge. "We had trouble getting gigs because we weren't good enough," Neil remembers. Their last engagement, on December 29th, was at St. Ignatius CYO (Catholic Youth Organization), a Catholic church and parochial elementary school on the corner of Corydon and Stafford, near Young's home. Although it was The Classics' last gig, Neil would return to St. Ignatius later, and the place would play a key role in his development as a performer. But even before the Classics' final performance, Neil was already formulating his next plan.

During his second attempt at Grade Ten in the fall of 1962, Neil met classmate Jack Harper. Jack, recently graduated from J.B. Mitchell Junior High School in the far western end of River Heights, was a talented athlete and avid sports fan. This, however, was not what drew Neil's interest. One day at school, in an attempt to get to know this strange character better, Jack told Neil that he played the drums. Further, Jack's friend Allan Bates played a pretty fair guitar. "Neil said he had a friend who played bass, and I knew Allan, so we decided to put a band together," Jack recalls. Even before The Classics' final engagement, Neil was putting together his next band. "Neil and I formed the first version of The Squires in my basement during the Christmas holidays of 1962." The name and the musical direction of the band were both chosen by Neil. With a twin guitar lineup, The Squires jumped head first into the popular guitar instrumental field. That was their specialty. Neil was even beginning to compose his own instrumentals, which the band promptly learned. The Squires would go on to become a popular fixture on the thriving Winnipeg music scene and, despite numerous personnel changes, would be Neil's longest lasting musical unit ever, taking him from Winnipeg to Thunder Bay and eventually to Toronto in the summer of 1965.

FOUR

THE SQUIRES SOUND

We started a band
We played all night.
Da dada da.
Oh Canada
We played all night.

   DON'T BE DENIED, 1973

With their sights set on the bustling community club teen dance circuit, The Squires rehearsed as often as school work would allow through the month of January 1963. For Neil, the year had begun on an optimistic note. He was the leader of a new band, with good musicians, and there were plenty of gigs for the taking if they could get a show together. The original Squires included Allan Bates on guitar, Jack Harper and then Ken Smyth on drums, Ken Koblun on bass, and Neil. Allan Bates lived in south River Heights and attended the recently opened Grant Park High School. He had begun playing guitar at a very early age. "My mom bought me a guitar in grade four. Actually, I wanted a bicycle but my mom didn't want me riding on the roads, so she got me a guitar," muses Allan. Classically trained, Allan had the technical expertise that Neil lacked. Neil had taken a few lessons but quit, discovering that he was able to teach himself much quicker. He had an excellent ear for melody and, despite his inability to read music, he could play what he heard. When asked to play a song unknown to him, he would first ask to hear it. He then played it back from memory. Where Allan played from his head, Neil played from his heart.

The two got on well together. "I'd go over to Neil's place on Grosvenor some afternoons," Allan remembers, "and we would sit on his couch in the livingroom and play our guitars together. When we weren't playing, we'd hang out on a Saturday afternoon at Winnipeg Piano. That was a great place. We'd get all those guitars down off the walls and try them out." Winnipeg Piano Company, located on Portage Avenue downtown, was the most popular musical instrument store in Winnipeg. Pianos and organs occupied the main floor but downstairs the walls were filled with guitars — Gibsons, Fenders, and Gretschs. Musicians used to hang out in the basement guitar department. Band business cards were posted on the wall along with the names of musicians looking for a group. The store's liberal payment policy encouraged many musicians to take up their instrument.

Problems soon plagued the embryonic Squires, however. Jack found it increasingly difficult to commit himself to the band because of his involvement in sports and school. So, in early January 1963, after playing a couple of local engagements including the Westworth Church teen dance, Jack's family church in north River Heights, he dropped out of the band. He and Neil remained friends after the split, and Jack accompanied The Squires to their engagements on a few occasions.

The Squires needed a new drummer and Allan had someone in mind, fellow Grant Park student Ken Smyth. "I used to play drums in music class at school and that's how Allan heard of me. They needed a drummer because their drummer couldn't make all the engagements. So Allan approached me at school to join them," recalls Smyth. "The Squires was my first band." Smyth got his music start at age thirteen on a set of drums his father bought him from a pawnshop. An athlete at school, Smyth nevertheless was willing to make the kind of commitment that Neil wanted.

The personnel now set, The Squires began rehearsing in earnest throughout January 1963. With Neil from Kelvin, Ken Koblun from Churchill, and Allan and Ken Smyth from Grant Park, The Squires had a wide base to draw on in south Winnipeg for engagements. This time, Neil felt he had the right combination and the right sound to really get somewhere in Winnipeg. "Smyth and Bates were good musicians," Neil recalls. "We had a pretty good band together."

Practices were held in Ken Smyth's parents' basement on Waterloo Street in south River Heights. Neil ran the practices, suggesting the songs the band would learn. He was the leader, though he did not command the others. His leadership was understated and understood more than exerted. He gained allegiance from the others because they respected him. Neil took practices seriously, and he made sure no one missed them. The sound emanating from the basement would draw friends and the curious from around the neighborhood. As word of the band got out, Smyth's basement became a hang out for school mates and young musicians. Duncan Wilson and Garth Nosworthy, two budding River Heights guitar players, used to sit in awe of Neil's playing. Inspired, they went on to form The Mongrels, one of Winnipeg's top bands in the late 1960s. "There would be a whole host of guys there when we practiced, listening and shooting pool," Allan recalls. "Neil used to play a lot of pool when we weren't practicing." Ken Smyth remembers Rassy visiting the house once during a practice and commenting to his parents about putting up with all the noise.

Mixing the current instrumentals of the day and ones penned by Neil, the musicians worked hard at learning enough songs to fill three sets. There was plenty of instrumental material to cover, including *Walk, Don't Run, Tequila, Wipe Out,* and *Telstar.* The only thing holding them back was their rather limited equipment. "We started with just junk," chuckles Ken Smyth. "The first equipment we had was homemade. Ken Koblun had built his own amp, and Neil and Allan built a big amp for both of them to use. Then, as the equipment got better, we sounded better." But not before the band blew out the speakers in Mr. Smyth's hi-fi after plugging all their guitars into it one day. "Neil cut the speaker cabinet for the homemade amp at an angle so that the speaker would aim upwards for more penetration into the crowd," Allan recalls, "It was amazing what we did with that equipment, especially when the other bands in town had Fender Bandmasters and things like that. We didn't have the money at first for those kinds of things." Even to this day Neil is well-known as a technical wizard among cult guitar players for devising his own "whiz box" amplifier, as he calls it in a recent interview in *Guitar Player.* He remains very meticulous about his guitar sound.

On February 1, 1963, The Squires made their debut at Riverview Community Club in south Fort Rouge, Ken Koblun's area. They drew a small but enthusiastic crowd of teens and received five dollars for their efforts. One dollar each with a dollar left for gas. Hardly an auspicious debut, but Neil was pleased with the response they had received. Hustling their respective areas of south Winnipeg for gigs, The Squires next played Grant Park High School. With Allan and Ken Smyth as local celebrities, The Squires would frequently play at the school over the next year and a half. Neil's neighborhood community club, Crescentwood, was next in early March. "I always liked playing Crescentwood," Allan remembers. "A lot of tough guys were around there but that was okay because they were our buddies." For their first engagement at Crescentwood, The Squires were paid thirty-five dollars. Pretty good money, they thought, for doing something you liked.

"We started doing community club gigs in our area," Neil recalls," and it wasn't too long before we had our own little following." Their first attempt at branching further afield came on

April 26 when The Squires joined a battle of the bands show at Nelson MacIntyre Collegiate in the Norwood/St. Vital area of east Winnipeg. These events were popular with teens, allowing them to see three or four bands at one dance. The bands enjoyed the competition as well. Usually a DJ hosted and judged, though the events were often little more than a popularity contest organized by the local area favorites. That night, The Squires failed to win the competition but attracted enough attention to earn some future bookings.

Once gigs became more frequent, the equipment problem became more acute. Small halls like Crescentwood and Sir John Franklin Community Club were okay for The Squires' homemade gear, but larger school gymnasiums were another matter all together. They just couldn't provide enough sound to fill those halls. For these gigs, The Squires would sometimes borrow equipment from Chad Allan and the Reflections. By 1963, Chad Allan and the Reflections were the undisputed top band in Winnipeg. They were a union of the best musicians from Allan's Silvertones, The Jurymen, and The Jaywalkers, and featured Chad Allan (Allan Kowbel) on guitar and vocals, Randy Bachman on lead guitar, bassplayer Jim Kale, drummer Garry Peterson, and Bob Ashley on piano. Neil fondly remembers Jim Kale's support of The Squires: "He let me use his Fender Concert amp. I thought I was in seventh heaven! He'd lend us stuff all the time. He was in a band doing a lot better than mine, yet it didn't bother him to help us." Ken Koblun would sometimes borrow Jim Kale's bass guitar. He also helped Ken buy his first Hofner bass. Neil remembers the incident. "Kale, Koblun, and I went to this appliance store where he ordered a bass. Cam's, I think it was called. I couldn't figure out why we bought it there." Rassy recalls Jim Kale being a frequent visitor to the house and often phoning for Neil. He was a talented bass player and, years later, Neil attempted to recruit him to join the Buffalo Springfield in Los Angeles. Kale passed on the offer, choosing instead to stick with his band in Winnipeg.

The Reflections were not only a popular band with fans, but an influential group among musicians. "Chad Allan and the Reflections were a big influence on us," Allan Bates recalls. "We used to go to some of their dances and Neil and I would watch Randy Bachman."

Randy was a tremendously talented guitar player and a musical trend setter in the city. He was extremely versatile, comfortable playing rock, country, jazz, even classical styles. Burton Cummings loves to tell the story of how Randy impressed Burton's mother and grandmother one evening while waiting for Burton to be ready to leave for a gig. "I had just joined the Guess Who and was still a teenager. Randy came to pick me up one night and, as usual, I wasn't ready yet. So he went out to his car and brought out a nylon string acoustic guitar and entertained my Mom and Grandma with Broadway show tunes. The guy was incredible. I was in awe of his talent." Randy had studied for a time in Winnipeg under jazz guitar great, Lenny Breau, who, in turn, had been taught by Chet Atkins. Even by age seventeen, Randy had absorbed these varied influences into his own fluid style.

While playing community clubs with Mickey Brown and the Velvetones in 1960, Randy came to the attention of Allan Kowbel. A year later, after Randy had moved on to The Jurymen, Allan approached him to join The Silvertones. What attracted Randy to Allan's band was their predominantly British rock 'n' roll repertoire. Allan had been importing records from overseas for years and patterned the band's sound after artists like Marty Wilde, The Hunters, Shane Fenton and The Fentones, and, in particular, Cliff Richard and the Shadows. The Shadows had carved out their own career, outside of working with Cliff, recording guitar instrumentals. For Randy, the opportunity to play Shadows' material was inducement enough. Hank Marvin, lead guitarist in The Shadows, was Randy's idol at the time. "The Shadows were completely different from The Ventures and The Fireballs," Randy recalls. "They played much classier, more melodic, not as noisy. They made beautiful music with their electric guitars." Randy became the first guitarist in the city to emulate Hank Marvin's style of guitar, even using a homemade echo delay system for Marvin's distinctive sound. With a change in personnel and a shift towards The Shadows' sound, The Silvertones chose a new name, The Reflections. Shadows — Reflections. Get it? Allan Kowbel became Chad Allan. They would later change the name to Chad Allan and the Expressions after an American group called The Reflections scored a 1964 hit with *Just Like Romeo and Juliet*. A year after that, the band went through a further transformation becoming The Guess Who, securing a North American hit with *Shakin' All Over.*

Neil speaks glowingly of Randy Bachman. "Randy was definitely the biggest influence on me in the city. He was the best. Back in those days he was years ahead of anybody else in the city. He had a homemade echoplex from a tape loop on an old tape recorder. He did that Shadows' style better than anybody else. He was playing a big orange Gretsch guitar and I got one like his. I still play an orange Gretsch like that one today. My heroes were guys like Bachman and Kale. I always thought Randy's guitar playing was great. I'm like an axe compared to him." Neil's acknowledgement of Bachman's influence can be found in the dedication on the back of the BUFFALO SPRINGFIELD AGAIN album in 1967.

Watching Randy playing with The Reflections, Neil was soon smitten with The Shadows' sound. "Were we influenced by The Shadows? Is the Pope Catholic?" laughs Allan Bates. "We just loved The Shadows. That was the major portion of our repertoire." Neil names some of The Shadows tunes The Squires performed: "We did *Apache, Wonderful Land, FBI*, and one called *Shindig*, I think. There was another one called *Spring Is Nearly Here* that we did. We didn't do any Cliff Richard stuff though, just Shadows." Fans recall other Shadows' numbers like *Dance On* in The Squires' repertoire as well as Link Wray's *The Rumble.* Neil was especially impressed with Shadows' guitarist Hank Marvin's use of the tremolo arm on his guitar. Marvin was the first British guitar hero, a bespectacled, studious looking musician who carefully picked out the echo-drenched melodies in all The Shadows' many instrumental hits and who unquestionably inspired hundreds of would-be U.K. guitarists to switch to a solid electric guitar. His red and white Fender Stratocaster, given to him by Cliff Richard, was the first ever Strat to have been imported into the U.K.

"Neil had an old Gibson Les Paul Junior guitar that used to give him shocks," Allan recalls. "One time we were in Smyth's basement practicing and Neil kept getting shocks from this Gibson. He just picked it up and threw it across the room and it smashed against the wall." Soon afterward, Neil acquired that orange Gretsch, like Bachman's. "I bought it from Johnny Glowa who was the guitar player in The Silvertones before Randy," states Neil. Rassy adds, "The guy couldn't keep up the payments on this Gretsch, so Neil paid him what he owed on the guitar." Neil debuted his prized guitar on September 20, 1963 at a dance at St. Mary's Church basement. Thus began Neil's life-long love of Gretsch guitars. He used them exclusively when playing in the Buffalo Springfield and the Crosby, Stills, Nash & Young bands. He still owns a number of extremely rare White Falcon guitars. Randy Bachman shares this appreciation for Gretsch guitars and owns the largest collection of these long-since out-of-production instruments, numbering close to three hundred models which he stores in a specially designed and secured warehouse. George Harrison's collection of Gretsch models is second only to Bachman's. Randy frequently rents his collection to other artists like George Michael for use in videos.

The next purchase was a new amplifier. He felt that his homemade one was inadequate for the band's sound, so, in a mood of optimism, he decided to ask his father for a loan of $600 for a new amp. Unfortunately, given the strained relationship between Scott and Neil, coupled with an unfavorable phone conversation with the principal at Kelvin indicating in no uncertain terms how poorly Neil was doing at school, the request was rejected. In fairness, Scott did hold out some hope, offering to consider the issue if Neil's June report card showed some improvement.

But for Neil, the need for a new amp was immediate, and in the end, Rassy bought one for him. "She bought him a good amp," Ken Smyth remembers. "We all went over to his place and we walked in and there was this big amp and we thought 'oh boy!' She was behind Neil, no doubt about that. He was her pride and joy."

The Squires quickly became a popular attraction on the Winnipeg teen scene circuit. "We played every church hall, school, and community club canteen in the city," states Ken Smyth. "I enjoyed playing the community clubs. It was a more relaxing atmosphere, just a lot of kids having fun and dancing." Neil adds, "We played River Heights Community Club a lot. We always drew crowds there. Glenwood Community Club was a big gig. We played there a few times." An engagement at River Heights Community Club was the pinnacle of success for local bands. It was the signal that you had arrived and were significant. Possessing one of the largest halls and stage areas of all the community clubs, the venue was regularly packed by Chad Allan and the Reflections, but The Squires were community favorites. A big attraction at Squires' shows was Ken Smyth's drum solos. Small in stature, but quite muscular, he could really lay down a heavy beat. "The three of us would stand back and Ken would beat those drums," recalls Allan. "All the kids would crowd around to watch." The Squires' lineup was augmented on a few occasions by Neil's friend from Earl Grey, Jim Atkin, on vibes and bongos, and saxophone player Greg Mudry, a classmate of Allan's from Grant Park.

As early as 1962, Neil had begun writing his own songs. At first, he composed guitar instrumentals. Listening to these early pieces, one hears a definite flair for melodic style that reveals his influences. "A lot of those early songs Neil wrote had a definite Shadows' twang to them," recalls Ken Smyth. "Neil played just by ear, but he wrote a lot. We'd get together at my parents' house to practice a couple of times a week and he would show up each time with a new song or two. He had piles of songs. Songs that we never even played." Allan adds, "I'd go over to Neil's place some afternoons and he'd play me a new song that he wrote. Even back then he had a knack for writing good tunes, good melodies, and lyrics." As Neil states, "I used to sit in my bedroom a lot with my guitar and write songs." He knew from very early on in his career that the key to success was to write your own songs. "You had to have your own sound," he states. As Rassy remembers, "His music didn't sound like other people's right from the beginning." Even today, Neil's "sound" is distinctive: during the recording of *Tears Are Not Enough*, producer David Foster asked Neil to sing his lines again because he sounded off key. Neil's response was blunt: "That's my sound, man."

Neil had a girlfriend who could read music, and she would transcribe his songs onto sheet music. Then he would sign the sheets, put them in an envelope, register it, and mail it to himself. In this way, he established a simple form of copyright. After his mother passed away in 1990, Neil found among her possessions a letter still sealed containing the transcribed sheet music to two of his early compositions. He had mailed it to his address on Grosvenor and she had kept it all these years.

By mid-1963, The Squires were beginning to draw crowds

throughout the city. Their popularity drew the attention of radio station CKRC, always on the lookout for new bands to promote. "The big thing was to get a DJ behind you," states Neil. "Bob Bradburn was there. He was our connection at CKRC." Although Bob's on-air slot was the mid-morning show, nine to noon, when teens were supposed to be in school, he was, nonetheless, a name around the city. Bob adopted the band, plugging their engagements on the radio and hosting their community club dances. On July 12, 1963, Bob arranged an audition for The Squires with CKRC recording engineer Harry Taylor at the station's tiny two track studio. Having suitably impressed Taylor with fifteen or twenty of their best instrumentals, he invited them back a week later for a run through of two of Neil's compositions, *The Sultan* and *Aurora*. Satisfied with these two songs, Taylor arranged a recording date for July 23. On that date, Neil Young made his first recording. Two months later a 45 rpm single, *The Sultan*, backed by *Aurora*, was released locally on the V Records label, quite a feat for such a young band. The company was more noted for its polka records by popular duet Mickey and Bunny Sklepovich.

The Squires were V's first and last foray into more contemporary sounds. The single received considerable airplay at CKRC. Both sides were Shadows' styled instrumentals with *Aurora* featuring Bob Bradburn's mysterious voice at the end whispering "Aurora!" Along with drumming duties, Ken Smyth hit a gong at regular intervals throughout *The Sultan*, an attempt at an Arabian feel perhaps. Both songs reveal Neil's progress on guitar, though nothing of the nimble fingers he would show on later recordings. "With *The Sultan*," Neil reflects, "it was good to have it out, but I hadn't got the *sound* I was after yet. It was my first recording session and I was just glad to be there for the experience. I was still searching for that right sound."

That summer, while the band awaited the release of their record, Neil, Jack Harper, Jim Atkin, and one or two other friends hitch hiked 145 kilometers east to Falcon Lake in mid-August. They took along their pup tents, intending to spend a week by the beach. Jack knew some friends who had a cottage there as well. As is upper most in the minds of teenage boys, they were looking to meet some girls at the resort. It was there that Neil met Pam Smith. Pam and her twin sister Pat, both from the East Kildonan area of Winnipeg, worked at Falcon Lake during the summer. Their parents had a cottage near the beach. Pat worked at the restaurant, while Pam was employed at the drug store in the resort community. Neil met her there. "He was a very sensitive and sincere person," recalls Pam, "and I liked that about him a lot. We got to know each other then, and we were walking on the way to the cook house one day and Neil asked me to go steady with him. I made the big announcement to everyone and it was wonderful. He gave me his Kelvin High School ring with a wad of tape on it to fit me." The two dated from August through to December 1963. Pat Smith went out with Neil's friend Jim Atkin during that time as well.

The holiday at Falcon Lake held many special memories for Neil. Like many events or people in his past, images from Falcon Lake surfaced years later in songs. One, *I'll Love You Forever*, was written about meeting Pam along the beach. Neil recorded it with The Squires a year later, though the song remained unreleased. "She was my first sweetheart," he confides. As well, Neil wrote and recorded a song entitled *Falcon Lake* in 1967. "Falcon Lake was an instrumental," offers Neil. "It was a memory of that time at Falcon Lake. It was written and done in the Buffalo Springfield time. It had Stephen Stills and I and Buddy Miles on drums, but we never finished it. I later used the melody from it for *Here We Are in The Years* on my first solo album":

Now that the holidays have come
They can relax and watch the sun rise
Above all the beautiful things they've done.
Go to the country; take the dog;
Look at the sky without the smog.

See the world; laugh at the farmers feeding hogs,
Eat hot dogs.

HERE WE ARE IN THE YEARS, 1968

Neil and Pam often walked by the water together. "We used to fantasize a lot," she relates. "He had a terrific imagination, it was like dreaming out loud. He really liked nature. We would talk about what it would be like to live on an island. He had a wonderful laugh but he didn't laugh that often. He was so intense at times." In the evenings, Neil and Pam, Pat and Jim, along with their friends would build a fire on the beach and sit around toasting marshmallows and talking. Neil always had his guitar with him and would strum chords softly, then sing a song or two. Everyone would listen as Neil played. Falcon Lake is noted not only for its sandy beach and gorgeous lakefront view, but also for its well groomed golf course. This was a further attraction for Neil, a golf enthusiastic since his early years in Pickering. Around this time, Neil had befriended Jim Roy, an avid golfer from Pine Falls, Manitoba. Jim, three years older than Neil, had moved to Winnipeg to try his luck at becoming a golf pro. Jim later moved into the top floor of 1123 Grosvenor, after the death of Neil's grandfather, Bill Ragland. Pat Smith later went out with Jim Roy. "I think Jim knew Neil's brother Bob who was a golfer too," offers Pat.

Pam recalls Neil's usual topic of conversation. "He talked about music a lot and about making it his life. He wanted to be successful but he didn't measure success in terms of a big bank account. He did it from his heart." Neil also shared a personal revelation with Pam that he was only then learning to come to grips with. "He told me one day on the beach that he had epilepsy. He told me not to be scared and what to do if he had a seizure." Neil had told few people about this. He had experienced symptoms over the past few years and had been alerted to the problem by his doctor. The Squires were not aware of his problem, but Allan Bates recalls a strange incident at that time, which may now be understood. "One day before a gig, Neil and I were driving down Grosvenor and all of a sudden we went off the road and hit an oak tree on the boulevard. Neil was driving and his eyes sort of went out on him. After a minute or so, we just backed up and went off and played the gig." It was likely an early symptom of epilepsy. Neil would not experience his first *grand mal* seizure until 1966 while with the Buffalo Springfield.

With their first recording pumping up interest, The Squires

resumed their increasingly busy engagement schedule that fall. On the September 2, the band was booked to perform at an outdoor teen promotional event for Topps Discount Department Store in west Winnipeg. They set up on the back of a Coca-Cola truck in the parking lot. "It turned out to be a really cold day," laughs Ken Smyth. "I looked over and Kenny Koblun was playing bass with big, bulky gloves on." Even more unusual was an intermission engagement the band played at a wrestling match in St. Boniface, the predominantly French-speaking community of Winnipeg. "That was funny," laughs Neil. "Big Jean St. Boniface versus Killer Kowalsky and us in the middle."

Other engagements that autumn included a stint at the notorious Cellar club in downtown Winnipeg. The Cellar was the antithesis of the clean-cut innocence of the community clubs. Dark, dingy, and reeking of forbidden pleasures, it was the kind of place you didn't tell your mother you were going to. Tucked away down an alley off Fort Street, The Cellar was a subterranean hangout for the tougher element in Winnipeg. Descriptions of the club were routinely punctuated with tales of knifings and under-age drinking. The Cellar crowd was not easily impressed. For these four high-school boys from upper-middle-class River Heights, descending the dark stairs to The Cellar club was akin to entering the depths of Hell. Ken Smyth remembers a girl standing on a table and taking her clothes off, and a fight erupting near the stage. "I just caught a glimpse of a beer bottle that came at me and smashed on the wall."

The Crescendos, contemporaries of The Squires, were frequent performers at The Cellar, and singer Glenn McRae offers a description of the club: "The entrance was in a lane. Just even going down that lane was an experience, like you were in New York going to some hidden club. It was like something you'd see on *The Naked City* TV show. It felt exciting, seedy, forbidden. There was a big red door with THE CELLAR on it and you went downstairs to the basement. It was pitch black and smoky. The walls were even painted black with a mesh chain-link ceiling and pipes hanging down. There were no decorations and no stage, just a little platform. People kept their liquor in brown paper bags. One night, some guy walked down the stairs, pulled out a gun and started shooting. Everyone hit the floor. He emptied his gun and then walked out. Guitarist Chris Anderson was stabbed on his way down the stairs one night."

Surprisingly, The Squires returned to the Cellar on a few more occasions. Another odd venue was Paterson's Ranch House, in Winnipeg's multicultural North End. Seeking to tap the new teen market, the owner hired The Squires to play the country music haven. "There was this band that used to play there at night called Bluegrass Bob and the Bobcats," laughs Neil. "That was a pretty wild place. They let us do our thing Saturday or Sunday afternoons. We had to really work hard to get paid."

The Squires also played at the trendy, upscale Town and Country nightclub on Kennedy Street downtown. Upstairs, The Towers supperclub was Winnipeg's version of The Copa, with performers like a young Barbra Streisand who had performed there a few years earlier. Downstairs, the Gold Coach Lounge had become a popular spot for the University of Winnipeg hipsters to congregate. The Shondels had recently completed a successful two year residency at the lounge, and it was booking other groups in an attempt to recapture the excitement. The Squires were thrilled to be sharing the bill with their mentors, Chad Allan and the Reflections.

But the staple gigs for The Squires remained the community clubs. The band drew large crowds to Norberry, Maple Leaf, Greendell, and Winakwa Community Clubs. Pam Smith accompanied Neil to many of these engagements. "I always had to help him carry his equipment," she muses. "I think he went out with me because I was cheap labor." She offers a glimpse of Neil on stage back then. "When he was playing his music, he had one leg that was kind of stiff and he would just move his knee back and forth, in and out, in time to the music. He didn't move around much on stage, but he moved that knee. He used to use his tremolo arm a lot, going 'twang' with it. He would get this tight smile every time he used it. You could tell in his eyes, it went right through his whole body. His guitar was like a part of him and he didn't feel whole without it." But Neil also kept an eye on his girl. "Once when he was up on stage playing, I ended up dancing with a guy a knew from the lake. I remember this twang coming from the stage and I looked up and Neil shook his finger at me."

Returning to Kelvin for Grade Eleven, Neil had become a celebrity with the release of The Squires' first record. *Et Cetera*, the Kelvin student newspaper, noted The Squires' rise to fame in its first back-to-school issue that September with a short feature, appropriately titled "Twang":

> *In our midst, we have a future recording star. Neil Young and the Squires, sponsored by* CKRC, *have made a recording on the Vee label. On one side is "The Sultan" and on the other, "Aurora". Neil plays lead guitar, while Al Bates is on lead ??? Ken Smyth on drums and Ken Koblun on bass. The record now being pressed in Montreal is expected to be released in the near future. The Squires now have a contract with* CKRC *for weekly Friday Night High School Dances this year. This is an up and coming instrumental group with a bright future.*

The Squires' first venture out of the city came that November when they traveled to Portage La Prairie, 80 kilometers west of Winnipeg, to play a high-school dance. On the way home late at night, Neil spotted a farmyard with unusually large rhubarb plants. He stopped the car, ran out to the yard, and picked a large leaf. Returning to Winnipeg, he went by Pam's house. Serenading her from outside her window, Neil woke her up to give her the leaf with a note pinned to it for her. The band also journeyed by bus, equipment and all, 400 kilometers north to Dauphin, Manitoba on December 13 for a gig there. It was their highest paying engagement to date: $125.

Getting to in-town gigs was often a chore for the band. "We only had two cars," Allan remembers. "Smyth's Dad's big Chrysler and Neil's Mom's little jellybean of a car. I don't think the heater worked very well and we certainly noticed that in the Winnipeg winters." Neil remembers those winters all too well. "In winter, we used to have to go out and warm up the cars before we could put the guitars in them because they would crack in the cold." In 1984 during the recording of *Tears Are Not Enough*, Canada's response to the Ethiopian famine crisis, Neil was asked by Winnipegger Burton Cummings if he still lived in California. He replied that he did. "I did my cold time," he smiled. Rassy recalls with humor watching

Neil and Ken put Ken's big bass amplifier in the back of her little car and then the two of them wrestling with it to get it out.

In early 1964, The Squires took a bold step forward when they began mixing their instrumentals with songs featuring Neil on vocals. The catalyst once again was The Reflections. "We were into The Shadows and stuff," Ken Koblun recalls, "and then we saw Chad Allan's group doing Beatles stuff and we thought that stuff was great." Allan remembers Neil's discovery of the Beatles. An enthusiastic Neil met Allan at Crescentwood just after the Beatles emerged. "Neil brought in a Beatles record and said, 'Hey, these guys wear their hair over their foreheads,' so he started wearing a Beatle cut." Allan adds that Neil generally favored black turtlenecks and pointy shoes. "You could kick the eyes out of a snake with those points," he laughs. The band soon began introducing Beatle songs at their gigs. "Neiler and Ken Koblun would stand in the living room and play those darn Beatle albums and try and copy them," laughs Rassy. "The first song that I ever sang in public was at Kelvin in the cafeteria," Neil recalls. "It was a Beatles song called *Money*. I think I also did *It Won't Be Long*." Rassy smiles as she remembers a photograph of Neil around the time the Beatles came out. "I've got this picture somewhere of a wedding or family gathering or something where everyone is looking at the camera and smiling except Neil. He's got his head turned the other way watching the Beatles on television."

The arrival of Beatlemania and the whole British Invasion to North American shores shook up the Winnipeg music scene like nothing before or since. The band scene virtually exploded with dozens of new groups, all emulating the Mersey-beat sounds, while the already established bands quickly adapted to this exciting new wave. The Reflections, first to jump on the Beatle bandwagon, traded in their Fenders and Gretsches for more Beatlish Rickenbacker guitars. During their stage act, when it came time for a Beatle number, CKY DJ Darryl B would come out on stage with a large comb and, to screams from the audience, proceed to comb each band-members' hair forward over their foreheads, Beatlestyle. Chad Allan and The Reflections succeeded in recreating the British Invasion sound on record in early 1964, covering Gerry and the Pacemakers' version of *A Shot of Rhythm and Blues* along with Randy Bachman's highly derivative *Stop Teasing Me,* a dead-ringer for Lennon and McCartney's *Do You Want to Know a Secret.* The Shondels rode the British Invasion tide with their recording of *Another Man*, a song that could fit nicely into the *Help* soundtrack, incorporating all the trademark Beatle hooks. Newer bands like The Crescendos followed the darker side of the British Invasion, the more rhythm and blues stylings of groups like Manfred Mann, The Undertakers, and Them. Crescentwood group The Orfans flawlessly covered the intricate Zombies' harmonies.

The Deverons, led by Burton Cummings, jumped headfirst into the British beat. "We were all big fans of the British Invasion bands," notes Burton. "I liked The Dave Clark Five, The Swinging Blue Jeans, and stuff like that." Deverons bassplayer Ed Smith became the envy of other musicians around the city when he imported a Vox amplifier directly from Britain. Longer hair and collarless Beatle jackets became *de rigueur* for local musicians. The Jury, who had been on the scene for a few years already, found it difficult to grow their hair to Beatle length because of their day jobs. No problem. They simply wore women's wigs when performing.

The Beatles themselves paid Winnipeg a fleeting visit in the summer of 1964. Although the city had been passed over for the Beatles first North American tour, their plane had to stop in Winnipeg for refueling. Hundreds of teenagers crowded the observation deck at Winnipeg International Airport for a glimpse of their heroes. When the Fab Four poked their heads out the airplane door, the screaming erupted. Deveron Bruce Decker took this as his cue and pushed past police security. Running up the stairs towards his heroes, he was quickly tackled by an alert Royal Canadian Mounted Police officer. The event, titled Decker's Dash, made all the newspapers the next day, making Bruce into a hero himself. Teen Dance Party host Bob Burns managed to approach John Lennon as the Beatle leader ventured a few steps down the stairs. "Hi, I'm Bob Burns from CJAY TV," offered Bob confidently. "That's your problem," snapped the cheeky Beatle. So went Winnipeg's encounter with Beatlemania.

Ken Koblun lived with a British family and had a direct line to England for British records, so, like The Reflections, The Squires were getting British records before they were released in Winnipeg.

"The British Invasion was a great, refreshing change," states Allan. "We played a job at Riverview Community Club when the Beatles were first out, and Neil got some real long Beatle wigs. We wore them out on stage and sang some Beatles stuff, and, boy, the girls sure loved that!"

Neil approached his new role as vocalist with the same resolve that characterized his outlook on music in general. It didn't matter what people thought of his singing, he was determined to persevere. "People told me I couldn't sing but I just kept at it." To be fair, his early vocal attempts did take some getting used to. "Neil would be singing at our house and we'd say, 'Oh, Neil, that's awful.' We were pretty cruel about his singing," laughs Jacolyne Nentwig. On one occasion, Ken Smyth's mother ordered the band from the basement to the garage due to Neil's screetchy vocals. At a gig at St. Ignatius church hall basement in January 1964, after their usual set of instrumentals, Neil announced that the band would attempt a song with vocals. Terry Gray was in the audience that evening and recalls the moment. "The band went to the back of the stage to put on Beatle wigs, retook their places and out came *She Loves You*. Nobody in the audience had ever heard The Squires sing, and they needed work." Someone in the audience boldly called out "Stick to instrumentals!" "Everybody said that Neil couldn't sing except me," claims Rassy. "I said 'It's an interesting key but if that's your key, who cares.'" Neil had found his "sound."

Presenting The Squires (above) in their official promotional photo. Back row — Neil Young (with his orange Gretsch guitar), Bill Edmundson. Front row — Jeff Wuckert, Ken Koblun (with his bass).

The Sultan, written by Neil Young and performed by The Squires, was recorded by V Records in September 1963, with Aurora on the B side.

V-109
Side A

45 RPM

"THE SULTAN"
by "The Squires"
Produced by Bob Bradburn

Harry Taylor (above) of
CKRC mixed and edited
The Sultan in his tiny
two-track studio.

The Squires were pro-
moted by DJ Doc Steen
of CKRC and performed
throughout the city of
Winnipeg at communi-
ty clubs, nightclubs,
and even wrestling
matches.

The business card
(opposite) for The
Esquires dates from
1961.

KELVIN ET CETERA

TWANG!

In our midst, we have a future
recording star. Neil Young and the
Squires, sponsored by CKRC, have
made a recording on the Vee label. On
one side is "The Sultan", and on the
other, "Aurora". Neil plays lead guitar,
while Al Bates is on lead ??? Ken
Smyth on drums and Ken Koblen on
Bass. The record now being pressed in
Montreal is expected to be released in
the near future. The squires now have
a contract with CKRC for weekly
Friday Night High School Dances this
year. This is an up and coming instrumental group with a bright future.

WATCH FOR THE CKRC
GUYS ON THE GO
AT THESE
EVENTS

Feb. 7—St. Mary's CYO
  Boyd Kozak
Feb. 7—Murdoch MacKay Coll.
  Doc Steen
Feb. 8—Portage la Prairie Indian School
  J. Paulson
Feb. 15—Melrose High School
  Jim Paulson
Feb. 19—Airways Community Club
  Bob Bradburn
Feb. 22—Selkirk Teen Hop
  Jim Paulson
Feb. 29—Selkirk Winter Carnival
Feb. 29—East St. Paul C.C.
  Bob Washington
Feb. 29—Melrose Park C.C.
  Bob Bradburn

ON THE GO RADIO
CKRC

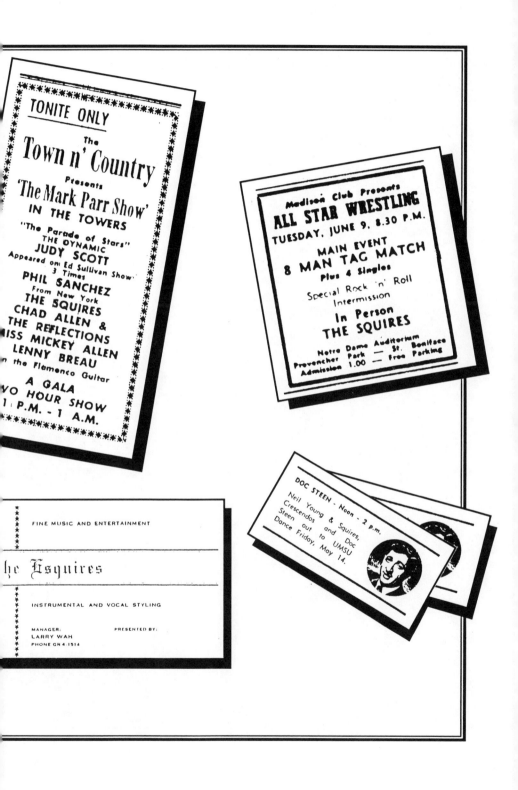

TONITE ONLY

The
Town n' Country

Presents

'The Mark Parr Show'
IN THE TOWERS

"The Parade of Stars"
THE DYNAMIC
JUDY SCOTT
Appeared on Ed Sullivan Show
3 Times
PHIL SANCHEZ
From New York
THE SQUIRES
CHAD ALLEN &
THE REFLECTIONS
MISS **MICKEY ALLEN**
LENNY BREAU
On the Flamenco Guitar

A GALA
TWO HOUR SHOW
11 P.M. - 1 A.M.

Madison Club Presents
ALL STAR WRESTLING
TUESDAY, JUNE 9, 8.30 P.M.
MAIN EVENT
8 MAN TAG MATCH
Plus 4 Singles
Special Rock 'n' Roll
Intermission
In Person
THE SQUIRES
Notre Dame Auditorium
Provencher Park — St. Boniface
Admission 1.00 — Free Parking

FINE MUSIC AND ENTERTAINMENT

The Esquires

INSTRUMENTAL AND VOCAL STYLING

MANAGER: PRESENTED BY:
LARRY WAH
PHONE GR 4-1514

DOC STEEN - Noon - 2 p.m.
Neil Young & Squires,
Crescendos and Doc
Steen out to UMSU
Dance Friday, May 14.

The door of The Cellar Club, one of the rougher clubs, in Winnipeg, where Neil Young and the Squires performed.

Bob Clark of The Squires made these drumheads for their first out-of-town gig in Churchill, Manitoba in April 1965.

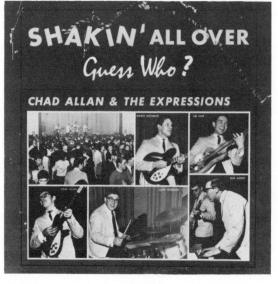

Winnipeg's premier band, Chad Allan and the Reflections perform at The Cellar in 1963, with Randy Bachman (center) playing his Gretsch guitar.

With the release of their first album in 1965, Chad Allan and the Expressions became the Guess Who? — and became internationally famous.

FIVE

FOUR STRONG WINDS

If our good times are all gone,
Then I'm bound for moving on.
I'll look for you, if I'm ever back this way.

FOUR STRONG WINDS, IAN TYSON

On February 5, 1964, The Squires achieved a minor milestone becoming the first rock 'n' roll band to play the Fourth Dimension, or "4-D," a folk music coffeehouse out near the University of Manitoba. The 4-D was the hip spot for the intellectual, beatnik, folk music, and poetry crowd. Popular attractions at the coffeehouse included Canada's answer to Pete Seeger — Oscar Brand — as well as Leon Bibb, Jose Feliciano, and folk-blues artists Sonny Terry and Brownie McGhee. By 1964, the impact of both the flourishing teen dance scene and the British Invasion had cut into the 4-D's drawing power. Neil convinced the management to take a gamble and hire his band to perform at the coffeehouse. "We went in playing Beatles stuff and jammed that place," recalls Ken Smyth. The enthusiastic response gave Neil further confidence in his vocal ability.

Neil was no stranger to the 4-D, having gone there a few times on his own or with friends to take in the folk fare and the hootenanies. Back in early 1963, the 4-D began hosting Sunday night hootenanies where anyone who wished could take to the stage in the center of the tiny, circular club and perform. Organized by Toronto singer Judy Orban, a regular at the 4-D, hootenany night became a popular attraction for the university crowd that frequented the club. With its drab tarpaper and snow fence decor, checkered table cloths, candles, and espresso coffee and cinnamon tea, the 4-D was the stereotypical bohemian coffeehouse. "I got into a Dylan thing in grade nine, playing folk," Neil recalls, "so I liked going to the 4-D."

At that time in Winnipeg, folkies and rock 'n' rollers did not mix. The folk crowd that inhabited the coffeehouses was largely upper-middle-class high-school seniors or university students who looked down their noses at rock 'n' roll. Because rock music dominated the airwaves, the folkies saw their music as elite, above mere pop ditties on the radio. There was more substance and message to their music. Certainly, they reasoned, there was more depth to *Blowin' in the Wind* than *She Loves You, Yeah. Yeah. Yeah.* In turn, most local rock 'n' rollers viewed folk music with a jaundiced eye, considering it void of excitement and emotion. Neil was a rare exception to all this, bridging the gap between the two disparate groups. He was a rocker who enjoyed folk music and was accepted in both camps. The Down To Earthenware Jug Band, composed of

Kelvin students, often entertained at the 4-D. Member John Robertson recalls Neil lending them a hand in their arrangements for songs, though he never performed with the group. Neil was already showing a leaning towards folk music, finding the lyric content much more meaningful and expressive than rock music's limited themes. What also appealed to him was the folk singer's ability to sing his or her own songs and have those songs stand on their own merit. Friends recall that Neil's favorite song around that period was Ian and Sylvia's folk classic *Four Strong Winds*. The song's theme, moving on and leaving loved ones behind in search of a dream, touched a nerve in Neil:

Think I'll go out to Alberta,
Weather's good there in the fall.
I got some friends that I could go to working for.
Still I wish you'd change your mind,
If I asked you one more time.
But we've been through this
A hundred times or more.

Four strong winds that blow lonely,
Seven seas that run high.
All those things that don't change,
Come what may.
If our good times are all gone,
Then I'm bound for moving on.
I'll look for you if I'm ever back this way.

FOUR STRONG WINDS, IAN TYSON

He would often sing that song at parties or among close friends, and later recorded his version of *Four Strong Winds* on his COME'S A TIME album in 1978. But in 1964, the 4-D became a haven for Neil between Squires' rock 'n' roll gigs.

Later that year at the 4-D Neil met a frail young folk singer from Saskatoon, Joni Mitchell, then working with her Detroit-based husband, singer Chuck Mitchell. Although Neil and Joni would meet again later in Toronto's Yorkville Village, the two would ultimately follow very different paths over the years to end up at the same goal, success as singer/songwriters in California:

Sweet Joni from Saskatoon
There's a ring for your fingers
It looks like the sun
But it feels like the moon.
Sweet Joni from Saskatoon
Don't go, don't go too soon.

SWEET JONI, 1973 (UNRELEASED)

Besides Joni Mitchell, Neil met Jesse Colin Young (later of The Youngbloods) at another Winnipeg coffeehouse called The Establishment where jazz guitar innovator and Winnipeg native Lenny Breau often played. Jesse Colin and Neil Young would meet again in Yorkville at the famous Riverboat coffeehouse.

Folk music had taken root early in Canada. Where rock 'n' roll was imported from the United States and Britain, folk music was very much a part of the Canadian culture. Combining the cowboy laments of the prairies with the traditional Celtic lilt of the Atlantic provinces, Canadian folk music was unique. Canadian folk singers didn't sing of civil rights marches or wars or protests. These just weren't Canadian themes. What folk singers across Canada did write and sing about was this country itself, the vast size and beauty of the nation, and their love of it. In his book *Heart of Gold*, an exhaustive history of Canadian contemporary music, rock journalist Martin Melhuish offers this assessment of the essence of Canadian folk music: "The vastness of the land and its space has been the inspiration for the poetic and lyrical portraits that have come from Canada's greatest folk singers and songwriters." Living in such a huge and beautiful country, how could they not have been inspired by what they saw around them? Just listen to Ian and Sylvia's *Four Strong Winds* or *Someday Soon*, or Gordon Lightfoot's *Canadian Railroad Trilogy* and you have a portrait of this land and its people. Drawing from the prairie yodels of Wilf Carter (a.k.a. Montana Slim in the U.S.) and Nova Scotia-born Hank Snow's *I'm Movin' On*, Canadian folk music has never been very far from country music, and folk singers here often achieve cross-over success in both markets. It was a natural progression for Ian and Sylvia from folk to country in the late 1960s. Few of their fans were even aware of the shift. Murray McLauchlan began his career in the Yorkville folk tradition as a kind of second generation Gordon Lightfoot, but has found far greater success in the country field without really changing his style. Lightfoot, himself, in his early days successfully bridged both charts, earning Juno Awards, the Canadian equivalent of the Grammy Awards, as a country singer/songwriter. Singer Marty Robbins took Lightfoot's *Ribbon of Darkness* to the top of the American country charts.

In the early 1960s, coffeehouses thrived in every city across Canada. What community clubs were to the neighborhood rock 'n' rollers, coffeehouses offered the same to local folk singers, a friendly place to listen and perform. What drew Neil to the 4-D coffeehouse in 1964 was the same thing that had been drawing young people to coffeehouses throughout Canada since 1960, an atmosphere and music that was intimate and expressive.

Even Canadian television embraced folk music, offering such popular shows as CBC's *Singalong Jubilee* and *Let's Sing Out* on CTV, hosted by Canada's folk music mentor, Winnipeg-born Oscar Brand. Toronto-based duo Malka and Joso offered multicultural folk music on radio and television on their *A World of Music* show. Buffy Sainte-Marie's blend of folk and country drew on her childhood experiences on the Cree Indian's Piapot Reserve in Saskatchewan's Qu'Appele Valley. Gale Garnett (*We'll Sing in the Sunshine*) and Bonnie Dobson (*Morning Dew*) both received their start on the eastern Canadian folk circuit. Joni Mitchell began her career singing at the Louis Riel coffeehouse in Saskatoon and the Depression in Calgary, before making her way to Toronto's Mariposa Folk Festival where she stayed after encountering the heady folk scene in Toronto's Yorkville coffeehouses. Yorkville, an artistic enclave amid the hustle and bustle of downtown Toronto, had a thriving folk music community that not only spawned many talented singers and songwriters but attracted them, too. Zal Yanovsky emerged from the Yorkville folk scene to form the Lovin' Spoonful in New York. Denny Doherty was drawn to that scene from Halifax, Nova Scotia, where he had sung in folk groups. He would eventually make his way south to join the Mamas and the Papas. In the earliest days of the Yorkville folk movement, Ian and Sylvia were the darlings of the bohemian coffeehouse crowd. Combining Ian Tyson's western Canadian cowboy roots and Sylvia Fricker's more traditional folk music sensibilities, the two forged a unique country-folk blend of Canadian themes and sweet harmonies. Many of their songs, like *You Were On My Mind, The Lovin' Sound, Someday Soon,* or *Four Strong Winds,* are considered folk classics on both sides of the border and are deeply ingrained in the Canadian cultural experience. Their sound soon outgrew the insular confines of Yorkville, and Ian and Sylvia headed south, thereby opening the door for other Canadian folk artists, like Gordon Lightfoot, across the border. Growing up in Canada, Neil was very much aware of folk music.

"Neil used to like hanging out at the 4-D," recalls Pam Smith. For Neil, the 4-D offered him more than food for his soul. Musicians who performed there ate for free. "Neil used to eat there a lot. When the band played there, we could have anything we wanted to eat and I remember something on the menu called a 'suffering bastard' but I never tried it." This unusually named delight consisted of a scoop of every flavor of ice cream on the menu in one sundae. Already, some people were taking notice of what Neil had to say in his songs, while still others ignored him. "I used to get angry sometimes when people talked or walked out while Neil was playing there because I felt that everyone should pay attention to him." Neil's own frustration with distractions during his performances is well known. He once stopped in mid song to berate a noisy patron at Carnegie Hall.

Neil was a frequent visitor to Pam Smith's parents' house and her Mom and Dad liked him. "Her parents had a grand piano and I would play it when I visited her," states Neil. "I was teaching myself to play piano at the time." Neil had promised that one day, when he was successful, he would buy Pam a red Corvette sports car. "So he gave me a little red Corvette dinky toy for my sixteenth birthday," smiles Pam. "I'm still waiting for the real one," she laughs. But in December, 1963, Neil and Pam split up. "He broke it off," recalls Pam. "I think he was afraid of a commitment. Even the thought of commitments scared him." The two remained friends afterward. "He asked me to go steady again months later, but I really didn't want to." On that occasion, Neil had picked Pam up at her home and the two went driving around the city, talking. Stopping at a Dairy Queen, Neil asked her to get back together with him. As they got out of the car he told her he loved her. Pam, just sixteen and unsure of how to react to such a bold statement replied in a fluster, "You love me, and I love ice cream!" Reflecting on her time with Neil, Pam states, "It had to be music for him. I don't know what else he would have done without music. He just loved it so much and was so committed to music. I couldn't imagine what else he would have become." She then adds, "He often felt frustrated that others didn't share the same dedication he had."

On April 2, 1964, The Squires again entered CKRC studios to record with Harry Taylor. This time, however, some of the songs included vocals. "I think we recorded a song called *Ain't It The Truth*, written by me," says Neil. "There were tapes of those songs around but they are probably lost now. We did about twenty songs." One song that did survive that session is *I Wonder*, the first recording of Neil Young's singing. Surprisingly, the vocals are quite good, in a very Merseybeat style popular at the time, complete with British inflections. One can hardly tell that this is the same voice that, years later, would be parodied as the voice only cats could love. The song is derivative of its period, sounding like a hybrid of the Dave Clark Five and the early Beatles, with a tough rhythm thumping throughout. It clearly shows that Neil had been absorbing the British Invasion:

Well, I wonder,
Who's with her,
Tonight.
And I wonder,
Who's holding her,
Tight.
But there's nothing I can say,
To make him go away.

Well, I never cared too much anyway.
Well, I guess that I'll forget her someday.

I WONDER, 1964

Neil's lengthy guitar solo in the middle eight bars reveals a maturity of phrasing, ending with a characteristic arpeggio tremolo twang. The song would definitely have turned some ears if it had been released then. Regrettably, it was not. However, Neil rerecorded *I Wonder* twice more during sessions later that year and again in early 1965, then adapted parts of the song in *Don't Pity Me Babe*, another unreleased number from late 1965. Still not finished with it, Neil resurrected *I Wonder* as the basis of his *Don't Cry No Tears* on his 1975 album, ZUMA.

During that same session, The Squires recorded an instrumental entitled *Mustang*. If *The Sultan* had been Neil's interpretation of The Shadows sound, then *Mustang* was Neil's tribute to Randy Bachman's own bow to The Shadows. Earlier, The Reflections had recorded a Bachman-penned instrumental, *Made in England*, which incorporated every hook, riff, and nuance of the distinctive Hank Marvin sound. The song was a tour de force for Randy's melodic, fast fingering. Randy even had the nerve to send a copy of the song to The Shadows themselves, offering it to them to record. "I still have the letter they sent to me," recalls Randy. "They said it just wasn't right for them at that time." Neil confirms, "*Made in England* was the kind of Shadows sound that we were trying to imitate." And he came very close on *Mustang*. "*Mustang* was really melodic," states Neil. "It's got a nice sound to it." Featuring busy drumming and intricate bass playing, Neil and Allan lay down fluid guitar lines that weave around the complex arrangement. Occasional stops and starts, as well as shifts in the chord pattern, give the song that Shadows' style. Clearly, both songs from this session show Neil Young's growing guitar talents, a sophistication in songwriting, and a clear statement of his influences.

Ain't It the Truth surfaced in 1988 when Neil resurrected the song for live shows with his band The Blue Notes. The song, as it was performed in 1988, demonstrates Neil's growing interest in rhythm and blues in 1964. Another song recorded but subsequently lost was the instrumental *Cleopatra*. It is also possible that one of Neil's earliest songs with lyrics, *No*, may have been performed for the session. "I remember writing *No* in my bedroom on Grosvenor," Neil recalls, "and I can still remember the melody. It was in the key of F." Ken Smyth claims that the 1964 recordings were for a proposed contract with London Records of Canada, but nothing came of it. After the session, Neil asked Harry Taylor his honest opinion of the material, and he replied, "You're a good guitar player kid, but you'll never make it as a singer." Years later, on a visit to Winnipeg, Neil dropped by CKRC. Harry did not recognize him until Neil introduced himself and said, "I came back to show you that you were wrong."

In the autumn of that year, a short Winnipeg newspaper feature entitled "Presenting The Squires" mentioned that the band was set to release another single, *White Flower*. "That's another one that I wrote, but we never recorded it," recalls Neil. "It was an instrumental that was supposed to be the follow-up to *The Sultan*. It was pretty cool." Rassy comments, "Neil wrote it about the assassination of President Kennedy. It had something to do with a white flower for peace or something. I remember it." So does Allan Bates. Backstage at Neil's concert in Calgary with Crazy Horse on his Ragged Glory tour in the spring of 1991, Allan picked up one of Neil's guitars and played *White Flower* for him.

The four members of The Squires, still in their teens and in high school, had become close friends. "We did everything together," offers Ken Smyth, "hung out together, dated together. After a gig we'd all meet at the Pembina Sal's restaurant or cruise over to the A & W drive-in restaurant." But by the summer of 1964, a rift was developing. The four were beginning to see music from different perspectives. "Neil was serious about a musical career early," reflects Allan, "so he quit school after grade eleven, on the advice of the principal who told him to go out and be a musician. He knew what he was good at and he went for it. We wanted to finish grade twelve." That August, Neil, Jack Harper, and assorted friends drove out to Falcon Lake to camp for a few days. While there, Neil convinced the hotel manager to hire The Squires to play at the resort, and phoned the others to come up to join him. Ken Koblun, always ready to follow his buddy, agreed. Ken Smyth and

Allan Bates had other plans and said no. "It didn't seem like a big deal to us, but to Neil it was," cites Ken Smyth. "Neil came back and broke up the band." The four fulfilled some commitments, then went their separate ways.

Looking back, Ken Smyth harbors only one regret: "It's too bad that it ended on a sour note. Neil was definitely upset when we broke up. Up to then, The Squires were a solid foursome. We had a lot of good times together." He adds, "To Allan and me, it was just fun. For Neil and Ken, it was their career."

After one month of school in the fall of 1964, Neil decided that his future was not to be found in the hallowed halls of Kelvin High, but as a full-time musician. There was nothing else that he wanted to do in life. Since junior high, he had considered no other vocation than music. He respected Allan Bates' and Ken Smyth's decision to finish school, but he couldn't relate to it. They had such a good thing going in The Squires. He thought it strange that the two didn't want the dream the way he did.

Rassy put up little resistance to Neil's decision to turn professional. "You only get one shot at it," she reflected, "and you had to do it when you were young." Nola Halter adds, "Rassy did want Neil to finish school but if that was what Neil wanted, then she supported him all the way." Scott Young, on the other hand, was not in favor of his son's decision. Neil had failed grade eleven, the result, his father reasoned, of too much time spent playing in the band. Scott believed there was nothing else for Neil to do but to knuckle under and do the year over. But he had little influence over his son and Neil went ahead and quit. In fact, the principal of Kelvin was supportive of Neil's decision, if perhaps for different reasons. He knew that Neil had no interest in school and only wanted to be a musician. "Go and give it a try," he told Neil, feeling confident that, once out in the real world, the young lad would quickly learn the value of a high-school education and come running back. Neil never did return, though among the photographs of illustrious alumni adorning the walls of the school is a picture of Neil. "He's Kelvin's most famous dropout," scoffed Rassy. Ken Koblun quit Churchill around the same time that Neil bid farewell to Kelvin.

With that decision under his belt, Neil now needed to find replacements for Allan Bates and Ken Smyth in The Squires. He didn't have to look far. Bill Edmundson lived across the street from Neil and had attended Kelvin as well. The two were already friends before the split in The Squires. Bill had begun playing drums in Montreal before his parents divorced and Bill came to live with his grandparents in Winnipeg. As he recalls, "We were really good buddies before I even joined the band. The band had folded and Neil was moping around. He came over one day and said 'I've fired everybody in the band. I need a new drummer, do you want to join?'" Bill accepted and promptly quit school. It was his first band. "When we went with Edmundson, we were really serious about making music our lives," comments Neil.

The next recruit was piano player Jeff Wuckert. A native of St. James in west Winnipeg, Jeff became the only piano player ever to be a Squire. "I was playing with The Concepts," he states, "which was the first band I ever played with. There weren't many piano players with bands around Winnipeg other than Mike Handford of The Shondels and Bob Ashley from The Reflections. We were playing a community club and Neil came to see us. Neil had heard of me and came to watch the band. He came up to the stage after and asked me to join them. Every one had heard of The Squires." At the tender age of sixteen, Jeff had already developed a reputation around the city for having backed Canadian teen idol Bobby Curtola. The move to incorporate piano represented a shift for Neil towards a tougher, more rhythm and blues sound. That style was Jeff's speciality and his piano playing added a new dimension to The Squires, if only briefly. Certainly, some of the songs The Squires had recorded that spring illustrated the blues style in Neil's writing. "By then I was listening to blues stuff like Jimmy Reed and getting into the harmonica," recalls Neil. Indeed, Neil became one of the first musicians in the city to use harmonica in a band. Glenn MacRae of The Crescendos remembers Neil teaching him how to play the harmonica during breaks at the Twilight Zone, a popular St. Vital teen club where Neil often hung out with other musicians.

Bill Edmundson's girlfriend Sharon worked at CKRC and arranged for The Squires to rehearse at their studio and have publicity photographs taken there. A few weeks later when a picture of the band appeared in the *Winnipeg Free Press*, Jeff was identified as Jeff Dack and Ken had become Ken Small, a ridiculous pseudonym for the six foot, five inch musician. "We used those names for a joke," muses Ken. Jeff explains, "Dack was my mother's maiden name and my middle name. I just decided to use it." Perhaps it was acknowledgement for the smart looking ascots and vests the band members sported in the picture, made by Jeff's mother. They would be the only outfits The Squires ever had and lasted even longer than Jeff's tenure in the band. Photographs of Neil performing eight months later reveal that same outfit. "I was never into stage clothes or fashion," offers Neil. "I was always behind everybody else in clothes." That certainly has remained consistent throughout his career.

Neil unveiled the revamped Squires at the 4-D. "We certainly played the 4-D a lot," recalls Jeff. "We practically ran the place. Neil knew a lot of the people that hung out there. Neil used to eat there a lot." For their debut, The Squires played for food, no wages. Friends state that Neil suffered from a chronic shortage of money. "He was always asking me for $2 for gas," states Jeff. "I think that's why we always rode with him. We used to go to the Red Top Drive-In Restaurant because all the bands hung out there and Jim Paulson would do live broadcasts from there for CKRC. But before we would go there we would drive to Paul's Hamburgers on Pembina Highway. They had cheap hamburgers, 19 cents each. Neil would buy four of them because that was all the money he had. Then we'd go to the Red Top and the rest of us would eat. He could never afford anything at the Red Top."

Even before he met Pam Smith, Neil had begun to date the Nentwig twins, first Jacolyne, or Jackie as she was known to her friends, in 1962 through 1963, then Marilyne by early 1964. "I could never tell the two of them apart," responds Ken Koblun in his droll manner. The girls knew Neil from Kelvin. Marilyne and Jacolyne had been regular dancers on Teen Dance Party on CJAY television as members of the "Pepsi Pack." "We used to go to all the schools throughout the city teaching teens the latest dances," Marilyne recalls. "Because we were identical twins, it was kind of a big deal." By the time Marilyne had met Neil, their public appearances were declining. Neil went with her once to the television studio for the show but declined to come in. He wasn't a dancer. The Nentwigs lived at 1111 Fleet Avenue in Crescentwood. When The Squires complained that they had no place to rehearse, Marilyne offered their basement. "My Mom said it was okay but she had no idea how noisy it would be, especially the drums. The neighbors went wild. It only lasted a week."

Despite this incident, Neil was a frequent visitor to the Nentwig home and always received a warm welcome from the girls and their parents. "Neil used to like being around our house," offers Marilyne. "I think he enjoyed being around a family, what with his family situation as it was. He was one of the nicer guys that we dated back then. He didn't eat us out of house and home like most guys did. The others would walk in and head straight for the fridge." Neil and Marilyne would spend hours together in the Nentwig's family room. "We really had a good time together but we never got into any trouble. We weren't bad kids. I always felt comfortable with Neil. I never had to fend him off. He was a gentleman and never made inappropriate advances. He was really cuddly, even though he was so skinny. He was very kind, sensitive, and romantic."

One example of Neil's romantic side came at a community club dance that Marilyne attended with him. "Going to these dances with Neil was never a terrific thing for me because I liked to dance and I couldn't because I was with one of the band. At this dance, I went to the washroom and there was a girl in there going on about how lucky I was to be going out with a guy in the band. I just thought, 'Boy, she's warped. I get to sit on the sidelines for the whole dance and help carry equipment afterwards!' I came out of the washroom and sat down on a chair beside the stage. Then, all of a sudden I was listening and I thought, 'Gee, that's not a song I've heard before.' I looked up at Neil on stage and he had a big grin on his face and he was singing the song *Be My Girl* that he had written for me. He had been working on it and didn't want me to know about it until that night."

Be my girl, be my girl.
Come on say you will.

When I saw you standing there,
With the wind blowing in your hair,
Then I knew that you'd have to be my girl.

Don't you know the way I'm feeling?
Don't you know that my heart's reeling,
For you, you, you, you.

Without you, life is not worth living.
All my loving, I'll be givin',
To you, you, you, you.
Be my girl.

BE MY GIRL, 1964

The Nentwig's had a Hammond organ in their home and Neil would often try to play it. "Neil would play the notes on the keyboard and Ken Koblun would play the bass notes on the pedals on the floor," recalls Marilyne. "Ken was really tall so he would be spread out across the floor playing 'boom da da boom da da boom' with the bass turned up loud. My sister and I took organ lessons but we were just learning and Neil would help us with the chords. Jackie wrote out the words to Neil's song *I Wonder* and Neil told us where to put in the chords over the words. We would all sit at the organ and play *I Wonder.*"

With The Squires now full-time musicians, the band needed their own vehicle. Neil had the solution, a second-hand 1948 Buick Roadmaster hearse. With enough room for all their equipment plus musicians, curtains to hide whatever was in the back, and a lift to load and unload easily, a hearse was the perfect band vehicle. Neil christened it Mortimer Hearseburg, or "Mort" for short, and it quickly became his most prized possession, next to his Gretsch guitar, of course. That hearse would go on to become an integral part of Neil Young's early image. Neil's father even wrote a column in the Toronto *Globe and Mail* about the hearse, using fictitious names rather than identifying his son as the source of the amusing story. Jacolyne recalls her first introduction to Mort. "It looked in rough shape. It truly looked like it wasn't going to make it very far." Her father was even less impressed. "He had a fit when Neil and Ken came over to our house to show us the hearse," laughs Marilyne. "He just said, 'What next!'" Indeed, what was next for Neil was heading out on the road.

Neil and Marilyne drifted apart once he left school. Marilyne remained at Kelvin to finish Grade Eleven. That autumn, Neil began dating Fran Gebhard who worked part time at the 4-D. A student at St. Mary's Academy, she had been one of those girls in the blue tunics that hung out at Stan's drugstore near Kelvin. She first saw Neil at a dance at St. Ignatius CYO. "Neil was attractive to all the girls," she smiles. "He was tall, dark, and played in a band. He broke my heart about three times, but I didn't mind. I was always willing to bounce back." Fran confirms Neil's perpetual poverty. "You knew that when you went out with Neil that you had to bring money. He never had any money. And you had to carry his equipment, too. A big date was Neil and I going to a Kelvin or Grant Park high school basketball game and then sitting in the car for three hours listening to him play his guitar." Fran chuckles over Neil's obsession with music. "We'd go to a party and everyone would be upstairs having a good time and Neil and I would be in the basement listening to him play guitar. He loved that guitar and he loved to play. All he talked about was playing music and writing songs. He never talked about being rich and famous, just playing all his life, doing something he enjoyed as his job."

Jeff Wuckert and his girlfriend Judy Wallace spent a lot of time with Neil that September and recall his preoccupation with music. "He used to hang around with us and tag along but he never had a steady girlfriend then. The girls he did date were never as important as his guitar! We would ride with him to gigs, the three of us, and Neil hardly ever talked. He never discussed anything. He was always in his own world. He didn't make small talk. He was always thinking about music. He was so different and he knew how different he was but he didn't care what other people thought of him."

Jeff's attitude towards a musical career clashed early with Neil's. "I wanted to play in a band but I never liked the lifestyle, the grubby clothes and casual habits. Neil did." The issue came to a head a month after Jeff had joined the band. On October 12, 1964, The Squires journeyed 500 miles east to Fort William,

Ontario. Now out of school, Neil wanted to move the band further afield. In terms of popularity on the Winnipeg scene, The Squires remained firmly in the intermediate level. Chad Allan and the Reflections, The Shondels, and The Jury occupied the top echelon and stood little chance of being toppled from their prominence among both fans and musicians. Bands like The Deverons, Crescendos, Luvin' Kind, Orfans, and Squires, although all experiencing city-wide popularity by then, were still no match for the top ranked groups. Below them were the hundreds of young bands who had yet to break beyond their neighborhood community clubs. Neil knew where he stood and the caliber of the competition in Winnipeg. He decided to look beyond the city limits. Few musicians in Winnipeg back then were daring enough to try their luck in another market. Neil and The Squires were. Their first tentative step was a trip to 'Fort Bill.' "We went to Fort William the first time without a gig," Neil remembers, "and we got one at the Flamingo Club." Because Jeff's father would not allow him to travel with the band, The Squires went as a trio. Neil would never return to Winnipeg for any prolonged period of time again. He was on the hard road to success.

SIX

LIVING ON SUGAR MOUNTAIN

Now you say you're leaving home,
Cause you want to be alone.
Ain't it funny how you feel,
When you're finding out it's real.

SUGAR MOUNTAIN, 1964

In 1964 Fort William, Ontario was the twin city of Port Arthur, located at the western tip of Lake Superior, just northeast of Hibbings, Minnesota, Bob Dylan's hometown. Amalgamated into one city called Thunder Bay in 1970, this urban area is quite sprawling, encompassing the original two cities. As a railway terminus, the skyline of both cities is dominated by enormous concrete grain elevators which store western Canadian farmers' wheat. Its port facilities on the lake handle large grain and iron ore ships moving resources out of the region to markets around the world. As an inland port, it is frozen over for five months of the year. Nestled amid the dense coniferous forests of the Canadian Shield region, the city is overseen by mysterious Sleeping Giant Mountain offshore on an island in Lake Superior. Besides grain, teen idol Bobby Curtola was the region's most famous export, having scored a series of national hits in the early 1960s. Bobby often worked the Winnipeg scene and his name was familiar to Neil. More recently, Thunder Bay's claim to fame has rested in the fact it is the home of Paul Schaffer, bandleader on NBC's "Late Night with David Letterman." In 1964, Fort William was an unglamorous, industrial city, but to Neil and the other Squires, it represented their dreams come true. Here they were, three teenagers out of school, playing in a rock 'n' roll band, on the road away from home. They could hardly contain their excitement. Neil saw great things for The Squires in Fort William. "I always figured that the biggest advantage we had was to be from out of town," he states. "We immediately got curiosity. We weren't somebody they had watched learning how to play. We were somebody who showed up out of nowhere that was doing something they hadn't heard before. That got everybody's attention." And indeed they did.

The Flamingo Club had seen better days by the time The Squires arrived. Located at 344 N. May Street in downtown Fort William, the Flame, as it was called locally, was known as much for its fights as its music. Owner Scott Shields was attempting to pump some life into the club but had fallen heavily into debt. Hiring the Winnipeg-based Squires was not going to revive his fortunes but their appearance did have an impact on the local music scene. The Squires were booked to play the Flamingo from October 12 to 17 for a fee of $325. Accommodations were provided at the Victoria Hotel on Victoria Avenue. The engagement was enough of a success to warrant Scott Shields' booking them for a two week return engagement in November with a raise to $350 per week. Neil, Ken, and Bill returned to Winnipeg elated with excitement over their first excursion on the road. Following a Hallowe'en dance at River Heights Community Club, The Squires departed the next day for Fort "Bill." That next trip would provide some important milestones for Neil.

When he left for Fort William that early November morning, Neil was still eighteen. His nineteenth birthday was quickly approaching, however, and he would be forced to spend it away from home. On November 12, 1964, Neil turned nineteen. The significance of reaching that age, his last teen year, almost twenty and an adult, coupled with celebrating his first birthday away from the comfort and security of his home and Mom, inspired Neil to write what many consider to be his most endearing song, *Sugar Mountain*. Alone in his room at the Victoria Hotel, Neil poured out his anxieties over impending adulthood, with its loss of childhood innocence, into the poignant lyrics of the song:

> *It's so noisy at the fair,*
> *But all your friends are there.*
> *And the candy floss you had,*
> *And your Mother and your Dad.*
>
> *Oh, to live on Sugar Mountain,*
> *With the barkers and the colored balloons.*
> *You can't be twenty on Sugar Mountain,*
> *Though you're thinking that you're leaving there too soon.*
> *You're leaving there too soon.*
>
> *Now you say you're leaving home,*
> *Cause you want to be alone.*
> *Ain't it funny how you feel,*
> *When you're finding out it's real?*

Oh, to live on Sugar Mountain,
With the barkers and the colored balloons.
You can't be twenty on Sugar Mountain,
Though you're thinking that you're leaving there too soon.
You're leaving there too soon.

SUGAR MOUNTAIN, 1964

Sugar Mountain was not added to The Squires repertoire. Neil felt at the time that it was too folkie for his band to perform, so he stored it away, awaiting the right time to use it. It would be a year before that time would come. The song has endured, however, in his solo live performances since the late 1960s and has tugged many heartstrings. On hearing Neil perform *Sugar Mountain* in 1965, Joni Mitchell was moved to compose *The Circle Game*, her own paean to lost childhood. Earlier in the week, Neil had written to his father telling him of the engagement at the Flamingo and his impending birthday. In the letter, he expressed his confidence in the band and a level-headed attitude towards where he wanted to go with music.

During that two week stand, the band was billed as "Rock 'n' Rolling Neil Young and the Squires, Recording Stars under the Vee Label." Neil's recent penchant for raucous sounding rhythm and blues songs was given full reign at the club. "We did *Farmer John* really good back then in Fort William," Neil recalls. "We used to break loose in it. That was one of the first times I ever started transcending on guitar. Things just got to another plane, it was gone. And the people would say, 'What the Hell was that?' We didn't even know what we were doing. People knew they had been watching a normal band playing these cool songs, then all of a sudden we went berserk and they didn't know what was happening." Neil was beginning to experience the pure physical exhilaration of music as a force deep within him. "There was this guy from Toronto named Garry from The Rubber Band. He could really play the Telecaster guitar well. He was there once watching us play *Farmer John* and we came off stage and he said, 'Where the Hell did you learn to play guitar like that?' He could play all the technical stuff and I didn't know what I was doing. We just got way out there and we were really playing. We just went nuts, Kenny, Bill, and I. That's when I started to realize I had the capacity to lose my mind playing music, not just playing the song and being cool." Neil would revive *Farmer John* for his RAGGED GLORY album and tour.

That November, Neil's songwriting not only reflected his folk leanings in *Sugar Mountain*, but also his rhythm and blues interest. The songs *Hello Lonely Woman* and *Find Another Shoulder* were two such rollicking R 'n' B numbers he penned at the Flamingo. They would not appear again until 1988 in The Blue Notes rhythm and blues live shows. Neil had forgotten them until Ken Koblun sent him some lyric sheets he found in a box a few months after their Blue Note Cafe reunion:

Well, hello lonely woman,
Won't you take a walk with me.
I know a place where we can go,
Grab a bite to eat.
Hello lonely woman,
Well, you're looking just like heaven,
On a clear, clean night.
I know you need me
Like a river needs rain.
I won't ask you any favors,
Until I pass this way again.

HELLO LONELY WOMAN, 1964

Donnie B and the Bonnvilles were the top band in the Fort William-Port Arthur area in 1964. However, they were big fish in a small pond, and took every opportunity to check out, and learn from, other bands when they passed through the area. "There weren't that many bands around here," recalls the Bonnvilles saxophone player Tom Horricks, "so when The Squires came to the Flamingo, we were interested in them because they were from out of town. Neil came in with this big orange Gretsch guitar that nobody had ever seen here. That really flipped a lot of musicians out." Another person who dropped by the Flame to see The

NEIL YOUNG: DON'T BE DENIED

Squires was CJLX radio DJ Ray Dee. Ray was a popular radio personality in town who worked with bands securing gigs for them. He also had a keen interest in recording and took every opportunity to bring bands down to the station to make tapes.

"I used to go in and use the studio at night," recalls Ray, "and bring in bands. I'd record almost every band that came through. Many of them got their first recording experience that way." On the night of November 23, 1964, Ray brought The Squires down to the studio on East Victoria Avenue to record some of Neil's songs. "We had to get the whole band into a very small studio," says Ray. "The session was primitive to say the least. All we had was a mono machine but the studio had the best acoustics and expensive Telefunken microphones. I had to set up Bill and his drums in the news booth and run the cables into the studio. We isolated the drums and the only reason we did it was because Edmundson was so damn loud. Neil was off in another part of the studio." Ray recalls Neil explaining the song he planned to record, *I'll Love You Forever*. "He told me that this song was about a girl he had met at a beach near Winnipeg. 'She was probably my first love,' he said. And the song goes, 'As I walk beside the sea' and 'I'll love you forever.'" Ray decided that the theme of the song required further embellishment. "We had an old transcription disk with the sounds of the ocean on it at the station. I mixed these sounds with the music and it sounded pretty good." Neil confirms that sentiment. "I really thought it sounded great. That's the first time that I felt I had made a recording that I felt that the feeling had come out. I was starting to get the whole recording thing. I even had a double tracked vocal on it." Ray thought Neil's voice needed more strength so he decided to double track it. "He wasn't singing as shrill as he later did around the HARVEST album. Maybe it was because of all the nights he had been singing here. It was a mellower sound."

Two separate takes of the song were laid down and kept by Ray. On one, the sound effects are used to cover a drumming mistake. The Squires also took another stab at recording Neil's *I Wonder* during the session. Ray's objective in recording The Squires was to have a demo tape to send to record companies in Canada to secure a recording contract for the band. He still possesses the master tapes to that sessions along with a rejection letter from

Capitol Records in Winnipeg who passed on The Squires' recordings. Neil offers this assessment of Ray Dee and his role with The Squires in Fort William: "When Ray was working with us, things seemed to be organized and together. Things were pretty cool. We had good gigs, we recorded. I really liked Ray. He was a great guy."

During their stay in Fort William, The Squires also played another club. The Fourth Dimension in Fort William was part of a chain of similarly named coffeehouses including the one in Winnipeg and another in Regina. The Fort William 4-D was the folk music bastion of the area, so naturally Neil was drawn to it. Located at the corner of Simpson and George Streets, the coffeehouse was the place where local musicians hung out. "The 4-D started out as a folk club," states Tom Horricks, "but it got rockier as time went on. The owner, Gordie Crompton, was really attempting to bring some kind of musical culture to this town. He was trying to bring some big acts to his club." Neil convinced Gordie to let The Squires play late afternoon "hootenanies" in exchange for food. Once again, the response the band received was positive and would have a profound impact on Neil's musical direction later. Neil determined to bring the band back to the 4-D, rather than the Flamingo, in the spring. He had something new in mind and the 4-D was the suitable place for his ideas. During that brief stint at the 4-D, The Squires befriended Terry Erickson, a local musician who often backed up entertainers at the coffeehouse. Like Neil, Terry shared an interest in both rock and folk music. As a bass-player, Ken and Terry found much in common. In fact, Ken had borrowed Terry's Fender bass and British-made Vox amplifier for the recording session at CJLX. The Squires completed their extended Fort William season on December 2 with an intermission spot for The Bonnvilles at the Fort William Coliseum. The trip had been successful and, as Neil and Ken headed home, they were already planning their return. Bill, on the other hand, had other things on his mind.

Returning to a bitter Winnipeg winter, The Squires now entered a period of instability that would not be resolved until their return to Fort William in April of 1965. Having tasted the road and lived the lifestyle of a traveling musician, Neil knew that his future in music was not going to be playing community clubs in Winnipeg. The Fort William experience had been a lesson in the realities of the professional music business. "At that point," Neil realized,"there really wasn't anything more important in my life than playing music." Neil had learned that to make it, you had to be prepared to make sacrifices — to leave home, to follow the scene. Neil was ready to do so. So was Ken. Bill wasn't.

Neil "fired" Bill Edmundson soon after The Squires returned to Winnipeg. "Neil fired Bill Edmundson because he was too unreliable," recalls Rassy. Neil offers his explanation for Bill's exit: "Bill was in love with a girl from CKRC whom he eventually married, so he wanted to be with her." Bill's girlfriend was pregnant and a hasty marriage was arranged. For Neil, releasing his friend was not an easy task. "The hardest thing I learned to do was to fire someone," offers Neil. "If somebody didn't fit in, I knew I had to tell him. Whereas if I hadn't have been so serious about music, I probably wouldn't have had to do that. But knowing what I knew, where I wanted to go, what I had to do, there was no way that I could put up with things that were going to stand in my way. I knew what had to be done to make it and you had to really want to do it and your music had to come first." Reflecting on Bill's reluctance to follow his dream, Neil offers: "Bill was there and was very much a part of everything that happened. It was just as important to him as it was to me, what the band was doing and everything. But he didn't share my determination to keep on going at any cost. He wanted to stay back where he knew things were okay rather than try for more. He was a wonderful person who loved to sing and play. He could have done what I did, but he didn't."

Over the next four months, a string of musicians came and went. Neil was in search of the right combination of musicianship and professional attitude. "I always believed I could find someone else that might have the determination. That's the only thing that kept me going was thinking that the next guy was going to share the same attitude that I had. I probably asked almost everybody in Winnipeg. I was trying to put together a band and I was looking for people who wanted to take a chance. Maybe that's why I couldn't find any. I think a lot of people wanted to go but couldn't." During this period, the drum stool was briefly filled by Kelvin schoolmate Terry Crosby, Al Johnson, and Randy Peterson, younger brother of

Guess Who drummer Garry Peterson. Neil approached Kenny Hordichuk of The Shondels but Kenny declined, choosing to stay with a more secure gig. Ken Smyth even sat in for a gig in Selkirk, Manitoba, to help Neil out in a pinch. Guitarist Doug Campbell, another Kelvin student, joined The Squires around this time. Doug had been a member of The Dimensions, Ken Smyth and Allan Bates' new band, until Neil lured him away.

"The best group was with Doug Campbell and Randy Peterson," states Neil. "That group was fine! Doug Campbell was so far ahead of his time. He just played so good! He was as good as Randy Bachman but nobody knew who he was. He was the first guy I knew who used really light gauge guitar strings so he could really bend them. He also had built his own fuzztone way back before there were any fuzztones. He was the biggest loss for the music world because he wouldn't pursue a career." This short-lived lineup also recorded. "There was somebody else in somebody's garage or basement in the North End of Winnipeg that recorded us," says Neil. "It was me and Koblun, Randy Peterson, and Doug Campbell. We made a record of a song called *(I'm a Man And) I Can't Cry*. I had a copy of the tape for years but I don't know where it is now. We got a pretty good sound. *I Can't Cry* was a rock song, not a ballad." The session also included a third try at *I Wonder*. Obviously, Neil felt committed to that song! He views this last attempt, with the Campell and Peterson lineup, as the best of the three recorded versions. It is believed that the sessions were again for Walt Grouschak at V Records, though nothing was ever pressed or released. Only one copy of the original tape remains in existence and surfaced recently with Ray Dee in Thunder Bay. "That was a great group," Neil recalls. "If we'd have played more shows, it would have been unbelievable. That group was as good as anything I saw when I came down to L.A."

This lineup rehearsed in the living room of Rassy's house on Grosvenor, much to the rancor of the neighbors. Complaints brought out the police: however, the officer who came to the door was himself a budding drummer and told Rassy and Neil to ignore the neighbors. He then asked if he could sit in on the drums. A new visitor to the rehearsals was teenager Diana Halter. Diana was the daughter of Nola Halter, panelist with Rassy on *Twenty Questions*.

"Rassy and my Mom were friends," offers Diana, "and Rassy kept saying, 'You've got to come over and meet my son. He and his friends have this group and they practice in my living room.' Rassy gave me Neil's little Baby Brownie camera to take pictures of the band. I could see their eyeballs rolling as I came in with this camera. So I followed them outside and took pictures of them loading the hearse before a gig." Diana started the one and only Squires fan club in March of 1965. "I would ask them all the inane questions like they asked in *Sixteen Magazine*, like what color do you like and what are your pet peeves. I would hand out typed sheets on the band at their dances."

Diana was a member of the River Heights Community Club Youth Council, responsible for booking bands for the weekly dances. "The Squires were one of the most popular bands at River Heights." She describes Neil on stage at the community club: "Neil didn't move around much on stage. His best friend was his amplifier, which he kept closeby. He was very concerned with the quality of the sound. You could tell that Neil had confidence in himself as a musician. It wasn't ego or contrived, he was very into the music. When I first met Neil, I thought he was terribly talented but I was afraid to admit it because his voice was so awful."

Randy Peterson was only fifteen years old when he played with The Squires. As the baby of the group, he took some ribbing from Neil. "Randy was cute," muses Diana. "Neil was always making jovial anecdotes aimed at Randy on the drums because he was the youngest." Randy recalls a few memorable tunes in their repertoire. "Neil used to do great Kinks songs like *You Really Got Me* and *All Day and All of the Night*. He loved all that hard rock stuff. He would do *Farmer John* and the rock 'n' roll stuff but we also did some old folk songs." Despite Randy's young talent, the inevitable crisis came. "Neil wanted to get out of Winnipeg but for me it was out of the question to go on the road. I was in grade nine! There was just no way I could follow him."

Prior to heading out on the road again in early April, The Squires' revolving drum stool was finally filled by Bob Clark. Bob hailed from Elmwood in the east end of Winnipeg. Just eighteen, he was a trained drummer who could read music. Bob's older brother Owen was a well-respected jazz and nightclub drummer at the time, and operated Clark's Drum Studio above a men's clothing store in downtown Winnipeg. "Bob had just broken into the scene," states Owen. "He was playing community clubs with two other guys when Neil saw him, and before we knew it, he was out on the road with The Squires." The band had received a booking in Churchill, Manitoba, some 1500 kilometers north of Winnipeg. In an increasingly familiar refrain, Doug Campbell's parents would not allow him to go on the road, so he was out. "He was a fine guitarist," Rassy remembers, "but his mother thought being in a band was the next thing to prostitution or something, so she wouldn't let him play."

As always, rehearsal space was difficult to find, but this new version of The Squires practiced at Clark's Drum Studio before heading north. Owen Clark recalls those rehearsals. "I had to leave by 7:00 p.m. to play at Chan's Moon Room. They would arrive at the studio around that time and rehearse as late as they wanted because they were the only ones in the building. I remember seeing them but I was into a whole different thing, jazz and standards, so I didn't care much for them. It was just a bunch of noise to me." One thing did impress Owen. "I was totally amazed at how they could go out and play a gig in ripped blue jeans and t-shirts! I was from the another school altogether, in shirts and ties." After a suitable period of rehearsal, "Neil Young and the Squires," as they were now billing themselves, left by train on April 7, 1965, bound for a week-long engagement at the Hudson Hotel in Churchill. This would prove to be the last Winnipeg-based Squires lineup. They never played a gig in Winnipeg. Neil's sights were now firmly aimed beyond the city limits.

For Bob Clark's mother Liz, the trip to Churchill came as quite a surprise. "I came home and there was a note from Bob: 'Gone to Churchill, see you in a week.' I was flabbergasted!" Churchill, like Fort William, was a grain terminus where western grain was loaded on ships bound mostly for the former Soviet Union. In recent years, the port facility has been declining in use and the existence of the town remains tenuous. The community was first established by the British-based Hudson's Bay Company as a summer port where the Natives of the area came to trade their beaver and muskrat furs for manufactured goods. After a long, cold winter on the traplines, the Cree Indians would trade their pelts for iron kettles, knives, blankets, and guns. The currency of exchange was pelts. Five beaver pelts were worth one iron kettle. For a rifle, the Natives were required to stack up enough pelts to equal the length of the gun barrel. The British constructed Fort Prince of Wales at the mouth of the Churchill River where it flows into Hudson Bay. The community grew around the old fort which still stands today. With the Bay frozen over almost eight months of the year, the winters are long and arduous in Churchill. Populated by the most rugged of individuals, any kind of entertainment is appreciated.

The lengthy train trip offered the young men a glimpse of the bleak Canadian tundra. "All the trees were leaning to one side with all the leaves on that same side," recalls Neil. "The cold north wind had pounded them down to nothing. They didn't look like trees but they were." Playing the Hudson Hotel proved to be quite an experience. "It was pretty hairy up there," Neil chuckles. "Playing in the Hudson Hotel in Churchill was like the Star Wars bar or something. There were half breeds, Indians, trappers, outcasts from society, big policemen with buffalo fur coats on, and maybe three women in the whole town. Every time one of them walked by, everybody went, 'Holy shit, did you see that!'" The frigid climate proved to be a formidable foe. "If someone really drank too much, someone else had to go home with them because if they passed out on the way home, they would die in the cold. One night they found an Indian guy half a block from the bar leaning on a telephone pole, frozen solid."

Despite these rigors, Neil was able to find some humor in their northern adventure. "I wrote a song to the tune of Jewel Aken's *The Birds and the Bees* that was about Churchill. It went, 'Let me tell you 'bout a thing called snow when it's forty-five below and a penguin I know.' I did it at the Hudson Hotel and it was a big hit. People loved it. I played it later for Stephen Stills in Fort William and he loved it too." Before bidding farewell to Churchill, The Squires experienced one last incident. "We were playing in the bar and the whole place started moving," laughs Neil. "A polar bear had crawled under the hotel and he was trying to stand up. It was warm underneath the hotel so it just burrowed through the snow. Everybody went outside and fired off guns and it ran away."

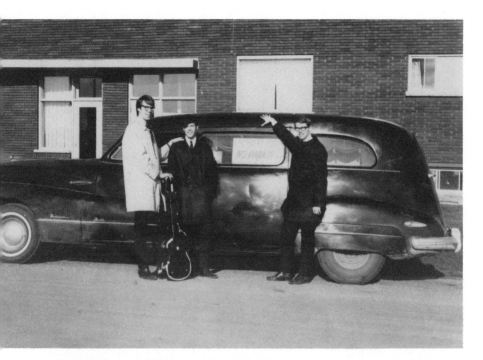

The Squires — Ken Koblun, Neil Young, Bob Clark — pose with Neil's beloved Mortimer "Mort" Hearseburg prior to departing for Fort William in April 1965 to perform at the Flamingo Club-Tavern.

BACK by Popular Demand TONIGHT

"ROCK 'N ROLLING" NEIL YOUNG
and THE SQUIRES

Enjoy the swinging music of Neil Young and The Squires,
just recently returned from an Eastern Tour. Recording
stars under the "Vee" label.

FLAMINGO
CLUB — TAVERN

344 N. MAY, ST.   DIAL 623-8458

*The Flaming Club-
Tavern welcomed Neil
Young and the Squires
back for a second
engagement, November
2-14, 1964. Neil wrote
the song Sugar Moun-
tain on November 12,
his nineteenth birthday.*

In May 1965, Neil Young and the Squires played at the "4-D" Club in Fort William where Neil first met Stephen Stills.

Neil Young and the Squires returned as celebrities to Winnipeg from their Fort William tours to play home clubs and schools, like this Valentine's Day Dance at Nelson MacIntyre Collegiate in 1965. Doug Campbell (right) on second guitar joined Koblun (left), Young (center), and Peterson (drums) for this gig.

SEVEN

LONG MAY YOU RUN

Well it was back in Blind River in 1962,
When I last saw you alive.
But we missed that shift on the long decline.
Long may you run.

LONG MAY YOU RUN, 1976

The Squires arrived back home in Winnipeg with just enough time to change clothes and pack Mort for another journey east. After the success of their short visit in the fall of 1964, Neil had determined to relocate the band to Fort William on a long-term basis. It was mid-April, 1965. As the hearse rolled down the highway through the flat Manitoba prairies, just emerging from the winter's snow cover, and into the rugged forests of northwestern Ontario, Neil had no idea that it would be six years before he would once more play in Winnipeg. The events of this trip would not only change Neil's life but would ultimately alter the course of popular music in the 1960s.

There was a great sense of excitement and anticipation among the three adventurers — Neil, Ken Koblun, and Bob Clark. Expectations were high. They joked about the previous week in Churchill, the polar bear incident, the strange people, and bemoaned the arduous train journey they had endured. They all agreed never to return to that remote outpost. Neil and Ken looked forward to renewing acquaintances in Fort William with Terry Erickson, Tom Horricks, Gordie Crompton, and Ray Dee at CJLX radio. When The Squires left Fort William in December, Ray had promised to line up some gigs in the area when they returned. In the intervening months since The Squires were last in there, Ray had been hustling their recording of *I'll Love You Forever* to record companies, but to no avail. Neil was carrying a tape for Ray from the recording session done a month earlier in that basement in North Winnipeg.

Bob Clark had only been a Squire for a few weeks but was adapting quickly to the transient lifestyle the other two favored. The trip to Churchill had been a "baptism by fire" for him. Already he had traveled farther afield than most of his contemporaries back in Winnipeg. Barely eighteen, this was all a merry adventure. Not so for Neil, who viewed their trip as the next logical step in his determined pursuit of a serious musical career. As always, Neil's mind was focused on music. For the first time he felt completely in control of his destiny. He was on the road, heading for "who-knows-what" but ready to tackle the unknown. As he drove, Neil recalled the words of Mose Allison's rhythm and blues song, "I live the life I love, and I love the life I live."

"Fort William is like a forgotten chapter in my life," cites Neil. "It had an immense impact on me because I really started to grow once I got away from home. It was my first big step on my own." Indeed, though Neil Young's career has been chronicled in the past, his experiences in Fort William, like those in Winnipeg, are consistently minimized. "Fort William was more important than Toronto for me in terms of my growth as a singer and songwriter. I gained a lot of valuable experience there."

On the trip, the trio talked of the recent success of fellow Winnipeggers Chad Allan and the Reflections. Renamed The Guess Who by early 1965, they had scored a Canadian number one record with their raunchy version of British rockers Johnny Kidd and the Pirates' *Shakin' All Over*. The song had even dented the American Top Twenty, and The Guess Who had embarked that same spring on a Dick Clark Caravan tour of the United States along with The Kingsmen, The Crystals, Sam the Sham, and other current hitmakers. The Guess Who had succeeded in breaking beyond Winnipeg, a point not lost on Neil. They proved that a group from the Canadian prairies could actually become successful internationally. Ironically, The Guess Who later became the first artists to cover a Neil Young song, recording his *Flying on the Ground Is Wrong* in early 1967. Neil was flattered that his old Winnipeg friends had recorded one of his songs. The Guess Who went on to earn international success in the late 1960s and early 1970s with hits like *These Eyes* and *American Woman*. Throughout their many ups and downs, The Guess Who remained based in Winnipeg.

Neil had decided that he had to leave Winnipeg. "It was a constant uphill battle to get gigs in Winnipeg. Finally, we decided if we wanted to get somewhere, we had to get out. At the time, everybody thought, 'What the hell are they going away for, this is it right here.'" His contemporaries on the music scene, comfortable in their celebrity status, chuckled to themselves that Neil would never be heard from again. But Neil was realistic about his chances for success in Winnipeg. "I always knew that I could never get to be the biggest band in Winnipeg. And I figured it was just as easy to become the biggest band in the country as it was to become the biggest band in Winnipeg. All you had to do was to go to where the biggest forum was and communicate with all of those people instead of the people in one city and just go and get in that race because in that city, you were from out of town. You have all the advantages of being someone unique that no one has seen before." But why Fort William? "Because it was halfway between Winnipeg and Toronto," he muses. Even then, Neil realized that Fort William was merely a stepping stone to where he really wanted to go, the center of pop music in Canada, Toronto.

The trip to Fort William was not without its mishaps. In order to save on gas, Neil would put his foot on the clutch and take the car out of gear, coasting down the many hills that lead to the city. "That's probably how I screwed up the transmission in the first place," he speculates. Owen Clark recalls hearing of the band's misadventures from his brother: "They had gotten somewhere on the road into Fort William and the hearse had broken down. They got out and started to walk. Bob told me later that they figured they were all going to die because the black flies were so bad that they were literally covered in them, biting and stinging. A trapper took them into a cabin for the night. Then he took them back the next day to fix the hearse."

The plan was to use the 4-D as a base of operations in the Fort William area. By playing afternoons and opening for headline acts, they would receive a room and as much food as they could nab from the coffeehouse kitchen. Gordie Crompton owned the 4-D as well as the Sea-Vue Motel off Cumberland Street. Out-of town-bands were given rooms there. The Squires occupied the corner room at the intersection of the two wings of the tiny, one floor motel complex. Crompton offered The Squires a simple arrangement. "They would split the take with me and played afternoons, breaks between acts, and Saturday jam sessions," states Gordie. "And they ate there for free." Like its namesakes in Winnipeg and Regina, the Fort William 4-D charged patrons by the hour. A time clock punched customers in as they arrived and when they left, they were charged twenty-five cents for each hour plus any food or beverages. The decor was similar as well, tar paper and snow fences covering the walls. Pepsi's were served calypso style, with a straw and a cherry. Patrons could even order a 'suffering bastard' there. It is no wonder that Neil and The Squires felt at home in the 4-D. "Everybody used to call

Crompton 'Dinty,'" muses Neil, who speculated somewhat imaginatively at the time that the nickname was drawn from Dinty Moore canned beef stew, a popular item for musicians on low budgets. Gordie Crompton explains the name somewhat differently: "I owned a Kentucky Fried Chicken restaurant named Dinty's so everyone knew me by that name. I got it for the restaurant by chance really. I went to a sign painter looking for a sign for the restaurant and he told me he had this sign that was never picked up and it said Dinty's. He said I could have it for fifteen dollars, so I said, 'Why not.'"

Neil recalls that "Dinty's favorite expression was 'I doubt it, Alice.' I used to say that all the time back then and that's who I got it from. The Sea-Vue was a pretty funky place. There was a store across the street where we used to go to buy Spam and crackers to eat." That room at the Sea-Vue was the scene of many late-night parties involving any musicians who happened to be hanging around or passing through town, along with any young ladies the band could lure from the 4-D after closing time. Inevitably, a jam session or sing along would ensue. Neil could never stay away from his guitar for too long.

Bob's mother Liz had some concerns over the band's spartan accommodations. "They were all living in one room in a motel and the conditions were not that great. Bob was a little dubious about being away from home and we weren't sure about it either. I think he was pretty homesick after a couple of weeks. The phone was always ringing, collect." Owen Clark adds, "Bob phoned me collect from Fort William and said, 'Can you send me $30?' They needed gas." Another frequent caller to the Clark home was Rassy who would phone to talk about the band and their problems in Fort William.

Once the word was out that Neil Young and the Squires were back in town, local musicians began dropping by the 4-D to renew acquaintances and check out their sound. There was a friendly competitiveness amongst the bands. "Because we weren't from Fort William, we were more interesting," offers Neil. "We were a step above most of the Fort William bands because it was a smaller town, and we were from Winnipeg." Neil had something further to offer the Fort William musicians, a new style of music he was about to unleash on the unsuspecting folkies at the 4-D.

On their first night back in Fort William, The Squires were scheduled to perform at intermission for an American folk group at the 4-D. This group, called The Company, made quite an impression on Neil and Ken. "We got in to Fort William Sunday night about nine o'clock," recalls Ken. "The Company had just finished its set, so we took about half an hour to set up our equipment before we played. We had some amplifiers that we had not yet tried out including an amp I had bought from one of the guys from Chad Allan and the Reflections. So we were a little nervous about our sound." Despite this concern, The Squires played well, impressing the young, blond-haired guitarist-singer for The Company, Stephen Stills.

"Neil was playing folk rock before anybody else," enthuses Stephen. "He had his big Gretsch, a rock 'n' roll band that had just turned from playing *Louie Louie* to playing the popular folk songs of the day with electric guitar, drums, and bass. It was a funny band because they could go right from *Cotton Fields* to *Farmer John*." Stills, a native of Dallas, Texas had spent much of his early years traveling. His father, a career diplomat, had moved the family from Dallas to New Orleans and even to Central America before settling in Tampa, Florida, where Stephen spent his late teens. There he joined his first band, The Radars. After high school, he drifted back to New Orleans to try his hand at folk singing in a duo with Chris Farns (who later became the road manager for the Buffalo Springfield) before making the pilgrimage to Greenwich Village, New York in 1964. There, Stephen remained on the fringes of the folk scene, working with noted singer/songwriter Fred Neil and hanging out with another novice folkie, Peter Torkelson. He joined a hootenany aggregation known as the Au Go Go Singers, a New Christy Ministrels-type minor league folk ensemble that played the eastern seaboard Ivy League college circuit. In that group, Stephen befriended Richie Furay, also recently arrived in New York from Dayton, Ohio. Richie had a remarkable voice with a clear, mid-western country-folk style that impressed Stephen. The two harmonized well and, soon after joining the troupe, they became roommates.

The Au Go Go Singers recorded one quickly deleted album of mundane folk standards of the time. Already Stephen was becoming restless; the music was too confining for his ideas. By 1965 more and more folkies were trading in their acoustic guitars for electric models and seeking out drummers and bass players to form groups. One such band of former folkies in Greenwich Village was The Lovin' Spoonful, led by expatriot Canadian Zal Yanovsky. After witnessing the formation and rapid rise to success of The Lovin' Spoonful at the Night Owl Cafe, Stephen determined that the future was not in folk songs but in electric folk-based rock 'n' roll. He had hoped to join the fledgling pop group but was never asked to audition. As Stephen tells it, "I desperately wanted to be in The Lovin' Spoonful. I was living in a hovel on the Lower East Side and I was watching this group getting together. They didn't know I could play electric guitar, bass, and drums. I wanted to be their bass player but they wouldn't give me the time of day. To them, I was just a kid wandering around The Village." The Spoonful's infectious brand of good time music was drawn from a quirky amalgamation of jug band folk and good old rock 'n' roll. Led by the homespun vocals and songwriting of John Sebastian and driven by the zany antics of Zal Yanovsky, their sound was unique and by 1965 was topping the charts from coast to coast.

After the full force of the British Invasion hit these shores, the Au Go Go Singers, and others like them, found themselves quickly out of favor with the public. The group split up in early 1965 and Stephen, along with a few ex-members minus Richie, formed a smaller folk unit called The Company. That spring, they arranged a short tour of Canadian coffeehouses. The folk scene was still hanging on in Canada and the coffeehouse circuit across the country offered a source of income for Stephen while he formulated his next move. So, on the night of April 18, 1965, Stephen and the Company found themselves the featured performers at Fort William's 4-D coffeehouse. And there, on the stage, was this strange rock 'n' roll band, with a tall, lanky guitarist-singer, wailing away doing exactly what Stephen wanted to do: electric folk rock. It was one of those fated, star-crossed moments in rock history, like the day John Lennon first encountered Paul McCartney at a Liverpool church-sponsored street party or the day Mick Jagger ran into Keith Richards, an arm full of blues albums at his side, on an East London train. On that night in Fort William, Neil Young first met Stephen Stills.

The preceding months leading up to the move to Fort William had been a transition period for Neil. During that time he began re-evaluating the musical direction he had been pursuing. Rock 'n' roll and rhythm 'n' blues were all right, fun to play, but not a distinctive enough style. Besides, he was beginning to write more complex songs with lyrics that transcended the typical 'boy-meets-girl-and-they-fall-in-love' sentiments of pop songs. He liked the more poetic, message-laden imagery of folk lyrics. He was being influenced increasingly by the folk singers he met as well as the music and lyrics of Bob Dylan. *Sugar Mountain*, the song he had written on that earlier Fort William excursion, showed a maturity of lyrics that revealed a shift away from rock to folk. Clearly, Neil was leaning consciously towards folk music, but he was not ready to abandon rock instruments. He still enjoyed the exhilaration of a driving beat and a loud electric guitar.

Neil had begun to experiment with folk music set to rock 'n' roll arrangements prior to the extended engagement at the 4-D in Fort William. What Stephen witnessed that night and subsequent nights after, before departing for the next city and the next coffeehouse, was Neil's early attempts at a merger of his two favorite styles of music, folk and rock. He would hone that style during the next few months in Fort William. "Fort William was the beginning of this kind of folk rock that we played," recalls Neil. "It was different from anything else I did before or after. It was a minor key folk, punk, rock kind of thing. It was funky."

Neil Young was by no means the first to attempt to merge these two music forms. The Byrds, not yet household names and having only recently changed their name from The Jet Set, were carrying out such experiments and had even recorded but not released the seminal folk rock anthem, Bob Dylan's *Mr. Tambourine Man*. Dylan himself was about to embark on his electric trip. His ground breaking single *Subterranean Homesick Blues* would launch an assault on the pop charts in May of that year, taken from the recently released LP BRINGING IT ALL BACK HOME. The album found the former king of protest ballads hedging his bets with one side acoustic folk, the other electric rock 'n' roll. Even The Byrds drew from other innovators like Los Angeles' Beau Brummels and especially Liverpool's Searchers. The latter are continually underrated in their influence on the origins of folk rock. Their recordings using electric twelve string guitar and tight folk-oriented harmonies in songs like *What Have They Done To The Rain* pre-dates *Mr. Tambourine Man* on the pop charts by at least six months. One can distinctly hear The Searchers' influence on the first Byrds album. Stephen's folk group, The Company, included electric bass and were moving in that direct when he encountered Neil. Clearly, others saw the marriage of folk and rock a worthy endeavor at the same time that Neil was taking his first tentative steps in this new idiom. There was something in the air that spring, and it would all break loose later that summer.

What made Neil's own brand of folk rock unique was his adapting of traditional folk standards to rock instrumentation. "We had a lot of songs that we were doing in that period that were kind of arrangements of other songs. We got into a thing in Fort William where we did classic folk songs with a rock 'n' roll beat and changed the melody," states Neil. "We did a really weird version of *Tom Dooley* which was like rock 'n' roll but it was in minor keys. And then we did *Oh Susannah* based on an arrangement by a group called The Thorns. Tim Rose was in The Thorns. We saw them at the 4-D. And also we did *Clementine* and *She'll Be Coming Round the Mountain When She Comes*. I wrote all new melodies. We changed them totally with rock 'n' roll arrangements. It was pretty interesting. It was different."

Watching The Company perform, Neil was immediately struck by Stephen's singing. "Stills' voice was phenomenal. His guitar playing was marginal. He was the rhythm guitarist, and he played a big red Guild acoustic guitar. He didn't really get into playing lead guitar until the Springfield. He was more of a singer. He had been with several singers in the Au Go Go Singers and the whole hootenany thing in New York so he was voice oriented, had voice training, and knew harmony." Neil's own knowledge of harmony singing was limited and he envied bands with tight vocal arrangements, like The Company and another band that passed through the 4-D that spring from Toronto, The Allen Ward Trio. "We had to spend hours working on harmony because we didn't know what we were doing," he laughs. "I knew what I wanted to hear and none of us really sang that good so our vocals were really funky. But we tried singing all of the parts in songs, any harmony, but we couldn't sing very well."

Following The Company's last set, Neil decided to introduce himself to Stephen. Tom Horricks of The Bonnvilles was with Neil at that time. "We were standing over on one side of the room watching The Company and Neil said, 'Come on Tom, let's go meet this guy.'" Tom hung back but Neil approached Stephen. Over the next few days, the two found much in common and enjoyed each others company, so much so that they talked of playing together. "We had a great time running around in Neil's hearse and drinking good strong Canadian beer and being young and having a good time," Stephen recalls. "At first I thought, 'Well, I'm gonna quit this idiot group and go play with him right now.'" The Company stayed at the Sea-Vue along with The Squires so it was natural that they hung out together, sharing music and good times. Ken Koblun developed a friendship with the female singer in The Company, Jean Gurney, who at the time was dating her group's bass player. After The Company left Fort William for a gig at the 4-D in Winnipeg, Ken continued to correspond with her. In their motel rooms, Neil and Stephen played some songs together, sharing their original compositions, but any plans to foster a more permanent working relationship would have to wait until The Company's tour ended. Then, with Stephen in the States already, Neil could join him there. "We got on quite well right away," remembers Neil. "We didn't talk about forming a band together then, but we knew that we wanted to get together later." Before leaving, Stephen gave Neil his New York address, where Richie was staying. "I knew he was going back to the States and I wanted to go to the States and now I knew a musician in the States." It would be almost a year, however, before their plans came to fruition.

As the weeks went on, The Squires became a part of the Fort William music scene. The loose atmosphere of the 4-D encouraged a sense of fraternity among the musicians in the city. Often during Squires' performances, friends would sit in with them. Tom Horricks sat in on occasion on saxophone as did Terry Erickson on either bass or rhythm guitar. Neil would frequently stay behind at the 4-D after closing time and just play his guitar, sometimes working out a new idea for a song. Monty Bond, who worked at the club, recalls many late nights listening to Neil play and sing. "He would drive me nuts," chuckles Monty, "playing the same songs over and over, trying to get them right." The Squires also hung out after hours at the downtown Tropics Restaurant in the basement of the Twin City Gas Building on Syndicate Avenue. Tropics owner Wayne Pang was a musician himself and, after serving the band some Chinese food, would convene impromptu jam sessions in the fourth floor hallway of the building in the wee hours. Wherever there was music being made, you'd find Neil. "I loved to play guitar all the time back then," he laments, "and now I don't even practice."

During this period, The Squires were drawing crowds who came to experience Neil's folk rock vision. "Neil was a curiosity piece," says Tom Horricks. "Every band in this area was envious of the Squires in a way because Neil was different. He was from out of town so everybody thought he knew something they didn't know. He was totally different from anything else happening then. He had a style. Neil was experimenting with original ideas and he had a lot of courage. He took heavy criticism from some people because everybody was so straight musically and here was this guy with this strange, high, reedy voice doing *Oh Susannah* with an electric guitar. Some people laughed at him but he wasn't afraid to be an individual. It didn't matter to him what anyone thought because he believed in himself."

Local radio personality Ray Dee managed to secure some one-nighters for The Squires between their regular afternoon and intermission stints at the 4-D. In May, the band performed at the Polish Legion Hall, Westgate High School, and a youth dance at St. Paul's Church in Port Arthur. These gigs were a refreshing change from the more sedate coffeehouse crowds and harkened back to the community club gigs Neil had enjoyed so much back in Winnipeg. At an out-of-town dance in Atikokan, a mining town northwest of Fort William, The Squires experienced Beatlemania-style fan hysteria. "When Neil and the guys came on stage," laughs Ray, "the kids screamed like it was the Beatles. They treated us like stars in that town." Ray also booked The Squires as the opening act for pop performers Jay and the Americans at the Fort William Colisseum. From rock 'n' roll *Tom Dooley* to *Cara Mia* must have been quite a shock for the audience!

On the last weekend of May 1965, Neil Young and the Squires were booked to play Thursday through Saturday evenings at the bar in Smitty's Pancake House, operated by the Circle Inn chain. They played the Thursday and Friday afternoon slots at the 4-D, then moved their gear over to Smitty's in the evening. For this series of engagements The Squires undertook a surprise name change. At Smitty's that week, crowds came not to see Neil Young and the Squires, as they had been billed since coming to the area, but The High Flying Birds. Neil explains: "The Company did an old folk song called *High Flying Bird*. It was a Billy Wheeler song. Stills sang it and he really sang it well. So we started doing our version of it. People started to tell us how well we did that song so we started calling ourselves The High Flying Birds." In fact, many people in the Thunder Bay area today remember The High Flying Birds more than The Squires. The name obviously caught on, and so did the song. A year later, The Bonnvilles, by then called The Plague, recorded a version of *High Flying Bird*, based on Neil's arrangement, on the Reo label in Canada and Crusader Records in the U.S. They also recorded *Farmer John*, again drawing inspiration from The Squires. By the time of the Smitty's gigs, Terry Erickson had become a frequent guest during the band's sets and there was talk of him joining the band as a rhythm guitarist. "We really liked Terry a lot," comfirms Neil. "He sat in with us a few times." As Terry recalls, "I liked the Squires because I liked folk music. I thought Neil's rock 'n' roll wasn't really rock 'n' roll. It was folk oriented. And Neil was a nice guy and very approachable." Don Baxter, the bartender at the Blue Swan bar, took some photos of The High Flying Birds with Terry, confirming his presence in the band. The four musicians posed with their instruments on some empty boxcars behind the 4-D.

Despite their minor celebrity status around Fort William, Neil, Ken, and Bob were barely surviving. Their regular spot at the 4-D was based on a percentage of the take and rarely netted the band more than $45. The Smitty's engagement paid $150 for the three nights. The one nighters they had performed were more lucrative, paying on average around $100, but these amounts were barely enough to keep the band alive. Transfusions of cash from Bob's parents and from Rassy came infrequently but were welcomed. Requests for financial assistance to Neil's father in Toronto continued to be rejected. With Neil now a full-time musician on the road, his relationship with his father remained cool. "I remember Neil phoning his Dad to ask for money while he was staying at our house," relates Monty Bond. "He was disappointed that his Dad wouldn't help him." Problems with Gordie Crompton over The Squires' antics at the Sea-Vue resulted in their eviction. Ken and Bob took rooms at the YMCA while Neil briefly stayed at Monty Bonds' house on Pruden Street before his mother sent Neil packing after failing to pay his rent. Monty's brother Harold was a local guitar player who knew Neil and The Squires. One afternoon, Harold received a phone call from Ken Koblun asking if he could fill in for Neil that evening. "Neil was tooling around in his hearse and it had broken down somewhere outside of town," states Harold, "and Ken asked me to come up to the Y to rehearse with him. But by the time of the gig, Neil made it back, so I didn't get to play." Soon after, Neil moved in with the other two at the Y.

Tom Horricks recalls a memorable incident with Neil at the Y. "I remember him and I on the second floor of the YMCA building and watching planes taking off and Neil turned to me and said, 'See Tom, they're just like big birds flying across the sky.' I remember that distinctly so that's where that line came from." The line he refers to appeared in Neil's song *Helpless*, recorded in 1970 by Crosby, Stills, Nash & Young on their hugely successful DEJA VU album. Although the song reminisces about Neil's childhood home in Omemee, Ontario, he does not deny that the line could have been from that incident in Fort William. "A lot of my songs come from images or flashes from things in my past, so it could have come from there. It's not specific in songs but you'll get scatters of images here and there that are about Canada more than a whole song. Very few of my songs are that specific."

In mid June, The High Flying Birds returned to play another weekend at Smitty's. As usually happened, various musicians and friends gathered after the last set on Saturday evening. Sitting around talking with the band afterwards were Terry Erickson, Tom Horricks, Ray Dee, and Donny Brown of The Bonnvilles. Their talk covered the usual themes of musicians on the road: music, girls, parties. But Terry had something more on his mind than idle chat. He had been offered a temporary gig with a band in Sudbury, Ontario the following week. He asked Neil if he would give him a lift to Sudbury in his hearse, a journey of some 650 kilometers around the coastline of Lake Superior. With little thought, Neil promptly agreed. It was a rare moment of impetuousness for him. Usually Neil considered decisions carefully before acting. "The only advice I ever gave him," confirms Rassy, "was to think. He never does anything without thinking about it very carefully." This time, however, Neil ignored his mother's advice and the spirit of the moment won out.

The drive from Fort William to the next major city, Sault Ste. Marie, is a notorious stretch of rock and tree lined highway winding through the rugged Canadian Shield region with few towns in between. What signs exist along the way warn drivers to watch for falling rock. The town of Wawa, approximately half way between the two cities, is noted for little other than the fact that it offers the traveler the last gas station and restroom for 350 kilometers. Billboards both entering and leaving the town make that point quite clearly. This would be no Sunday drive in the country. Neil and his fellow voyagers grossly underestimated what lay ahead of them. The events that unfolded from this casual request would ultimately become a major turning point in Neil's career. Neil would not return again to Fort William for twenty-seven years, not until May 92 when he received an Honorary Doctorate of Music from Lakehead University.

That Saturday night as Neil and friends discussed the impending trip, a youthful sense of adventure swept through them. Ken had already returned to the Y and knew nothing of their departure until the next day. When he did learn that Neil, Bob, and friends had left, he was miffed but anticipated their return later in the week to fulfill another weekend at Smitty's. Bob was all for the excursion. For him it was just another experience. He had nothing to lose. Ray backed out because of his commitments at CJLX radio, but Tom and Donny joined the merry crew. "The intent was just to drive Terry to Sudbury for a gig and come back," says Tom. "We wouldn't have gone along if Neil wasn't coming back. Donny and I had to be back for a gig the next weekend and so did Neil and

Bob." Neil confirms their motive: "We all decided just to go for the hell of it. Koblun didn't even know we were going. No one knew we were going other than the five of us. We just left that night. You know when you're that age nothing matters. We all just said, 'Let's Go!'" In hindsight he offers this assessment: "We really screwed up." Neil asked Ray for a loan of $30 for gas on the trip. Terry loaded his equipment into the back of the hearse along with his Honda 90 motorbike. Neil also took along his guitar and amp, a strange action if he was intending to return, but one needs to understand Neil at that time. He rarely went anywhere without his Gretsch guitar and would not pass up an opportunity to jam, even in Sudbury. So, in the early morning hours, with borrowed money, a motorbike, various guitars and amplifiers, the five young musicians embarked on their adventure.

At first all went well. The hearse rolled through the night and into the next morning. Neil was in his glory, driving his beloved Mort in the company of a group of fellow musicians. The first omen of impending disaster came near Sault Ste. Marie. Tom relates what happened. "We were in the back of the hearse, Donny, Bob and I, and I remember hearing this knocking going on underneath the back end. Now I'm getting concerned. Neil and the others were all laughing away like it's a big joke. So we get to Sault Ste. Marie and go to a garage station. The guy tells us we'll be fine. We were all sitting in the back eating Kentucky Fried Chicken and people were coming by and staring at us in the hearse like the corpses had come to life."

With a clean bill of health, Mort was on its way again, but not for long. Outside of Ironbridge, Ontario the vehicle lurched to an abrupt halt. Tom continues the tale. "Finally this knocking got louder and louder and then the transmission dropped out, steaming, onto the middle of the highway. I was saying, 'I think we're in trouble guys.' Neil and the others got out, looked at it, and started laughing hysterically." Neil recalls with puzzlement now the frivolous attitude he and the others initially took over the incident. "I don't know why but we were killing ourselves laughing. Here was my car, my whole life was in this car, falling apart on the road and we're rolling around laughing. I don't know why 'cause it was a sad thing but we could hardly stand up we were laughing so hard. And we weren't on any drugs or anything like that." Once the hilarity ceased, the five realized they had a serious problem. So Terry pulled the motorbike from the back and he and Neil went off to get help. At a nearby farm, they managed to phone for a tow truck.

When the tow truck arrived, the driver hoisted the broken down hearse from behind and began the journey to Ironbridge. However, he must have been in some kind of hurry to get home. With the front end down and facing backwards, the youthful adventurers, with the exception of Terry, sat in their vehicle watching the countryside flash past them. As the truck drove faster and faster, Neil began to panic. "The guy was pulling us so fast and the scenery was flying by us. I was trying to steer and I got really scared and uptight." Terry followed the tow truck on his motorbike. As the terrified occupants in the hearse sat in panic over the speeding tow, Terry was behind them showing off, doing figure eights and "do-nuts" on the bike. But as the speed picked up, he receded further into the distance. Then the motorbike stopped and Terry began waving frantically to the others as they, too, disappeared over the horizon. He had run out of gas. Terry was forced to push the bike a mile or so before discovering that it had a reserve tank. Red-faced, he caught up with the rest of the crew later in Ironbridge.

That first night, the musicians stayed at the Rod and Gun Hotel in Ironbridge. There was no adequate vehicle repair shop in that town, so the plan was to tow the hearse to Bill's Garage in Blind River the next day. That evening, in the bar at the hotel, Donny told Tom that they should pool all their money. "Donny says to me, 'Tom, we gotta give Neil all our money because he's in trouble.' Donny had about $40 and I had $80, so Neil had a big wad of bills in his pocket." The money was to be used to repair the hearse. The next day they were off to Blind River, this time with Tom behind the wheel. "I think Neil must have thought I was making fun of him or something on that first tow because the next day when the truck towed us to Blind River, Neil made me steer it and I think he must have paid the driver to go even faster than the day before. I was just shitting." The tow truck deposited the vehicle and its shaking passengers at the junkyard just outside of Blind River. Bill's Garage assured them that a new transmission could be located in a few days. So Neil and the others settled in to await the repairs.

The five weary adventurers slept in the hearse for the first few nights then took a room at a nearby motel. "There was a graveyard across from the junkyard and a motel sort of between the two," recalls Tom. "We rented one big room with about seven beds in it and we were all telling ghost stories. Donny says, 'I'm going to get that loose cross off that grave up there' and Erickson's yelling 'No, Donny, don't do it' cause he's getting scared. Then we would take Terry's motorbike one at a time up to the top of the hill near the graveyard. As you get up there, the light from the bike scans over the tombstones. Then we would drive like hell down the hill and the rush with all those tombstones behind you was just wild!" The presence of these long-haired, wildly attired young musicians caused quite a stir in the nearby town. "I used to take the Honda to the country store down the road and buy potatoes," recalls Terry. "We would go out to the graveyard and build a fire and roast potatoes. The local police came by once and told us to stay out of town because we were scaring the local residents." Tom adds, "It was like the Ozarks, only in the middle of Ontario. They had never seen long hair or wild clothes and here was Donny with long black hair like Injun Joe from Lil' Abner and wearing a cape. Terry had on a World War II German helmet with no lining so that it fell down over his eyes. Neil wore his usual jean jacket." Only Tom and Bob looked half way normal.

Neil remembers another misadventure. "I remember we were going to make a dam in the ditch by the side of the highway and flood the road, just for a lark. The police came by to ask us what we were doing." Terry picks up the story from there. "The cop asks Neil who we were and Neil replies, 'We're nabob poachers.' And the cop says, 'What's a nabob?' and Neil turns to me and says, 'See Clem, told you there were no nabobs here.'" The recounting of this particular story twenty-five years later brought gales of laughter from Neil. "We were young and just having fun," he concludes.

As the days went by and no transmission had been found, the group decided to split up. Bob, Tom, and Donny determined to make their way back to Fort William. Neil and Terry stayed behind with the hearse. "The hearse was more important to Neil than the gig back at Smitty's," states Terry, "so we stayed to get it fixed."

Having given Neil all their money, Bob, Tom, and Donny were forced to hitch-hike back to Fort William. "We had a terrible time on the way back," relates Tom of their journey home. "We were hitch-hiking and no one would pick us up because we really looked rough and Donny had this long hair. We walked thirteen miles from Wawa. We starved and stayed in a lumber camp for awhile. Finally we made it to White River and Donny and I wired our manager to send us the money to get home because we had to play on the weekend. He sent us the money but wouldn't pay for Bob, so we helped Bob get back. Then later, we heard how Neil and Terry had stayed in hotels after we left and ate steak dinners, with the money we gave them!"

Neil and Terry stayed on a few more days at the motel in Blind River. "Neil was writing songs all the time there," recalls Terry. "I've never met a guy who could write so much. He was sitting on the bed one day with his guitar and I was watching a spider make its way across the room. By the time it had crossed the floor, Neil had finished a song." The two then made the decision to abandon the hearse temporarily and head out on the motorbike for North Bay where Terry's father lived. Terry had hatched a wild scheme to convince his father to cash in some of his savings bonds to finance a trip for the two musicians to England. When they arrived, Mr. Erickson turned them down. The two decided that their next move was to make the journey south to Toronto to visit Neil's father. Perhaps, Neil thought, Scott would help him out this time and, besides, he wanted to see his father again. But they took a brief musical diversion before leaving North Bay. "I had some friends in a band there and Neil and I sat in with them one night. We also did a radio interview there, me, Neil, and Bob Steel who is an announcer on CBC radio. I think we even played a song or two on the air."

With Neil on the back of Terry's motorbike, the two lit out for the bright lights of Toronto. For Neil, there was no other choice but to keep going. He would keep in touch with Bill's Garage until a new transmission was found and then return to rescue Mort. He couldn't go back to Fort William without his hearse. The "Fort Bill" period, a time of growth and maturity for Neil musically as well as personally, had come to an abrupt end in that junkyard in Blind River. The next phase of his journey was about to begin in Toronto.

EIGHT

THE YORKVILLE SCENE

Back in the old folkie days,
The air was magic when we played.
The Riverboat was rockin' in the rain.

AMBULANCE BLUES, 1974

In late June of 1965, Terry Erickson and Neil arrived at his father Scott's home on Inglewood Drive in Toronto's posh Rosedale district. They were quite a sight having abandoned the hearse, for the time being, in Blind River and driven the Honda motorbike from North Bay, an uncomfortable journey of over 350 kilometers. "We looked pretty rough when we arrived at Scott's door," Terry recalls. "It was an impressive house. When we came in he offered us a drink. Then he pushed a button and a hidden bar opened up. I had never seen anything like that. He was very friendly but very businesslike. There wasn't a closeness between Neil and his dad, but he was courteous and offered to help us out." The two weary travelers stayed at Scott's for a few days. They had shipped their instruments and equipment by train and it arrived a few days later. Now, using his estranged father's home as a temporary base of operations, Neil began to check out the Toronto music scene.

Although there were healthy music scenes in Canadian cities like Winnipeg, Vancouver, and Montreal in the 1960s, Toronto was the center for Canada's music industry. The Winnipeg music scene, compared to Toronto's, was like Liverpool was to London in the early 1960s: an out-of-the-way provincial setting that spawned some talent (The Guess Who, Neil Young, BTO) but never eclipsed the pre-eminence of the music capitol. The major record labels were headquartered in Toronto and the top management and promotion companies operated from the city. Its pre-eminence in Canadian television production also furthered its prominence in the entertainment field. It was a well-accepted fact that if you were a hit in Toronto, you were a hit in Canada. Toronto became the mecca of the Canadian music industry. Not much has changed since then. For Neil, the trip to Toronto was not only a pilgrimage to Canada's music mecca, but also a return to his home. He had been born in Toronto and spent the first fourteen years of his life, the happiest years in fact, in or near that city before his family split up. In his continuing quest for musical acceptance, Neil's move to Toronto was the logical next step. "I was ready for Toronto after Fort William. The music scene there was the logical extension of what I was trying to do in Fort William," he states.

The "scene" of Toronto music at that time was the Yorkville district. Within the downtown Yorkville village district, a two block stretch between Avenue Road and Yonge Street one way, and Davenport and Bloor Streets on the other side, some ten to fifteen different coffeehouses could be found amid the closely-knit artistic community that thrived there. On any given night one could easily hear the strains of Eric Andersen, Tom Rush, or Odetta wafting from these tiny enclaves. These coffeehouses were literally houses, old, brick two and three story homes with folk singers or small groups performing in the front room or basement. Kids would crowd into these dimly lit rooms like sardines in a tin, spilling out into the hallways and stairs. Most popular of these were the Purple Onion, the Penny Farthing, the El Patio, Chez Monique, and the granddaddy of the Toronto folk scene, the Riverboat. Established by folk music impresario Bernie Fiedler, the Riverboat on Yorkville Avenue, was *the* gig for local folkies trying to get a start, as well as a major venue on the North American folk circuit. A young Joni Mitchell, having followed the coffeehouse circuit from Alberta to Toronto, was gaining a small but loyal following in Yorkville by then, especially at the Penny Farthing and Purple Onion. Living in one of the dozens of communal pads on Huron Street in the village, Joni perfected her songwriting craft in the coffeehouses at night, working during the day at a Simpsons-Sears department store to pay the rent. Her situation was hardly unique as many other aspiring folk singers inhabited the district. Her unusual guitar tunings and lilting voice drew the attention of those in the know who tipped her to be a future major talent. Unfortunately, not enough people took notice of her genius to keep her in Canada. By the time Neil had arrived in Yorkville, Joni was already married to American singer Chuck Mitchell and would soon depart Toronto for a base in Detroit.

Long before the term "hippie" was coined, restless youth, long-haired transients, and middle-class runaway teenagers from all corners of Canada drifted to Yorkville, drawn by the allure of freedom that the bohemian scene offered. There they mixed with the resident artistic community creating a colorful and heady atmosphere. Folk music was the common denominator for the strange inhabitants of the flop houses and communal pads of the district. By day, they occupied the street in their colorful garb "making the scene"; by night they congregated in the coffeehouses and dug their favorite folk singers. It was Canada's very own miniature Greenwich Village: hip, cool, artsy, and trendy.

Gordon Lightfoot was the crown prince of the Toronto folk scene, having accepted the mantle from Ian and Sylvia who had departed earlier for the real thing, Greenwich Village. Lightfoot's songs embodied the spirit of Canada: the railway, the prairies, lakes and forests, the despair in the cities. Lightfoot spoke the inner feelings of this land and its people. "Gordon Lightfoot's lyrics happened to say more to Canadians about Canadians than all previous movies, plays, and books put together," states Yorkville folk music impresario and manager Bernie Finkelstein. Lightfoot remains the quintessential Canadian songwriter and a national treasure. By 1965, his stature was outgrowing Yorkville. His songs had already been covered by more prominent folk artists and his star was rising. Peter, Paul and Mary recorded *For Lovin' Me* and Ian and Sylvia paid him their greatest compliment by making his *Early Morning Rain* a folk hit, and, in so doing, spreading his name to the more lucrative American market.

But by the late summer of 1965, the sounds of folk music were "a-changing." Bob Dylan had stunned longtime devotees by plugging in a Fender Stratocaster and striding on stage at the Newport Folk Festival that summer with a rock 'n' roll band. HIGHWAY 61 REVISITED, his first all electric album, was about to be released. The marriage of Dylan's stream of consciousness lyrics with electric instrumentation was a potent musical force to reckon with. A song from this album, *Like A Rolling Stone*, was quickly displacing the Rolling Stones' *Satisfaction* as the anthem of that summer. The Byrds version of *Mr. Tambourine Man*, complete with jangling electric twelve string guitar and a rock beat, was finally released and rocketed to number one on the pop charts. "When I got to Toronto," recalls Neil, "things were really happening like the Byrds' *Tambourine Man*, Simon and Garfunkel's *Sounds of Silence, House of the Rising Sun*. The folk rock thing was starting to happen." That autumn the airwaves would be dominated by the new folk rock sounds of originals like The Byrds and The Mamas and Papas as well as those who jumped on the bandwagon such as The Turtles, Grass Roots, We Five, and Sonny & Cher. The marriage of folk and rock which Neil had been experimenting with in Fort William was becoming a reality. His spirits were buoyed by these events and he began to formulate plans to regroup The Squires in Toronto. Like in Fort William, Neil once again saw his advantage in being the unknown commodity, the outsider, that would attract curiosity. However, Toronto was not Fort Bill.

Toronto had another face to its music scene that could be found amid the bright lights of busy downtown Yonge Street in places like Le Coq d'Or and The Colonial. These were the rock 'n' roll bars and they were the opposite of the sedate coffeehouses of the village — smoky, beery, loud, raucous music, go-go girls in tight mini-skirts and white go-go boots perched in cages adjacent to the stage, Fender Telecasters wailing. Here, a unique blend of southern rhythm and blues and primitive rock 'n' roll ruled. Gordon Lightfoot may have been the crown prince of Yorkville but on Yonge Street he bowed allegiance to the undisputed king of Canadian rock 'n' roll, Rompin' Ronnie Hawkins. This transplanted Arkansas redneck had turned Toronto on its ear in the late 1950s when he invaded the northland with his raucous rockabilly sound. He and his Canadian band The Hawks, driven by the incendiary guitar of sixteen-year-old Robbie Robertson, were a phenomenon, and had spawned many local imitators. One block but light years away from Yorkville's serene *If I Had A Hammer*, Ronnie Hawkins launched a blitzkrieg assault with *Bo Diddley* and *Forty Days*. Torontonians embraced both scenes, but never the twain did meet. At least not by 1965.

Although folk rock was the latest pop music trend on the airwaves, Toronto was slow to offer its own version. "I didn't see much folk rock in Toronto," recalls Neil. "It was either folk or rock." True to his love of both, Neil was comfortable in either venue. "In Yorkville I saw the Allen Ward Trio, who we had met in Fort William, Lonnie Johnson, Sonny Terry and Brownie McGhee. In the go-go bars I saw bands like The Sparrow who were great, and Luke and the Apostles. These bands were into rhythm and blues." The Sparrow began as Jack London and the Sparrow, a pop-oriented group that capitalized on singer Dave Marden's (a.k.a. Jack London's) English accent when the British Invasion hit these shores. That band briefly included on bass a seventeen-year-old Bruce Palmer who would play an important role in Neil's life and in the music of the Buffalo Springfield. By 1965 The Sparrow, minus Palmer, had flown the coop from Jack London and, led by an East German émigré named John Kay, were a hot item for local blues fans. After failing to garner much attention in New York in 1966, The Sparrow migrated to San Francisco but remained on the fringe of the Frisco scene until a name change to Steppenwolf and a song by former member Dennis Edmonton (under the pseudonym of Mars Bonfire) brought them success. The song was *Born To Be Wild*, the original heavy rock anthem, conceived by an urban Canadian kid.

The Hawks had defected from Hawkins' nest by the time Neil hit Yonge Street. Working the same juke joint circuit as Hawkins, Levon and the Hawks — namely, Levon Helm, Rick Danko, Richard Manuel, and Garth Hudson, along with Robbie Robertson — had released a couple of Canadian singles on their own to little attention. Unbeknownst to Neil, The Hawks first single had been recorded under the name The Canadian Squires in late 1964 on Toronto's Ware label. But the same summer that Neil arrived in Toronto, The Hawks were rehearsing there with Bob Dylan, readying themselves to provide the musical backup for the chorus of booes that was Dylan's first electric world tour. Later, renamed The Band, these four Canadians along with American drummer Levon Helm would go on to change the course of music history when, after a suitable period of writing and "woodshedding," they released the seminal album MUSIC FROM BIG PINK. Robbie Robertson had progressed far beyond the guitar hero title he wore in the Yonge Street taverns to become one of music's most gifted storytellers with a unique ability for crafting songs that vividly portrayed the bygone days of the American south a century earlier. Quite an accomplishment for a lad from the tough end of Toronto who quit school to follow Ronnie Hawkins. But Rompin' Ronnie had a waiting list of young recruits as long as Yonge Street itself. He continued to hold court at Le Coq D'Or Tavern when Neil hit town. Although Ronnie still likes to tell the story of how Neil was thrown out of the Coq D'Or for having long hair, Neil, in fact, admits that he never did see Ronnie Hawkins perform back then.

Another Hawkins protégé was also making a lot of noise in the bars. David Clayton Thomas, with his bands The Shays and later

The Bossmen, was a fixture on the Toronto rock scene. His 1966 release *Brainwashed* predates punk rock by a decade. Its buzz-saw guitar and venomous snipe at the Vietnam War were more than enough to keep it off the American airwaves. Nevertheless, it was a Canadian hit. But like all good Canadians of that era, the burly singer headed south to strike up a lucrative relationship with pioneering jazz-rock fusionists Blood, Sweat and Tears in the late 1960s.

Neil moved among all of this, absorbing the sights and sounds. He was equally at home on Yorkville or on Yonge. For him, the timing was right. He had a backlog of his own songs, was writing prolifically, and had a definite idea of the sound he wanted, folk rock. No more *Farmer John* and *High Heeled Sneakers*. Terry: "There was so much happening musically in Toronto. It focussed our attention more and made us more serious and showed us that we really had to have it together in Toronto." But first Neil needed a band. Within a week of his arrival in Toronto, Neil phoned Ken Koblun and Bob Clark who were languishing in Fort William. He had left Ken behind that night at Smitty's without word of the Blind River adventure. Bob had been forced to endure terrible hardships hitch hiking back to Fort William with Tom Horricks and Donny Brown after the breakdown. Some fences needed mending. Ken emphasizes, "Neil left Bob and I high and dry in Fort William." In fact, Ken was left holding a cheque in advance of the next weekend engagement at Smitty's. In need of money to live, he had cashed it, fully expecting Neil to return and the band to fulfill the commitment. When Neil failed to show, the marquee outside Smitty's read "The Birds Have Flown." With Bob back, the two were at a loose end, scraping by on the cashed cheque for a gig they never played, until a phone call from Neil.

"Something happened between Kenny and I," reflects Neil. "He was pissed off at me. I left without saying anything to him because we left on a lark. But I wouldn't have blown off the Pancake House gig if it hadn't have been for the hearse breaking down. It was a decision whether to abandon the car and go back with nothing or leave everything there and stay until the hearse was fixed. For the band and our whole thing in Fort William, the hearse had a lot to do with it. I just couldn't go back there without the hearse."

Neil offered his explanation for the current circumstances and begged Ken and Bob to come out to Toronto. He painted a rosy picture of the opportunities open for them if they could just get the band together. And he offered a further inducement. Neil had made contact with a well-connected manager in Toronto. Things were really going to happen for them, Neil stated confidently. The dream was still there, and perhaps now within their reach. Apologies accepted, the two sidekicks agreed to make the journey to "Hog Town." However, like the Blind River fiasco, this trip too was not without its misfortunes. "Bob and I only had enough train fare to get to Sudbury," recalls Ken. "We stayed at the Salvation Army hostel there until Bob's parents sent some money. If it hadn't been for Bob's parents, I would have starved to death there." Shipping their equipment on ahead by train, the two hitch-hiked the remainder of the way to Toronto.

"We met Neil at his Dad's place in Rosedale, but I just spent mealtime there," recalls Ken. "That night I went down to the Yorkville village where I knew someone, Elyse Weinberg. In order for me to get a place to stay, I offered to help them paint their apartment which they were doing at the time. I was on a ladder in the stairs and I stepped down to freshen my paint brush when the ladder slipped and I fell from the top stair and broke my little finger. That was my first night in Toronto." That incident should have served as an omen for the band. Things would only get worse.

With Terry now formally in the band, The Squires began rehearsing for their Toronto debut. Ken's finger was in a cast, limiting his playing ability. "I ended up playing a unique Framus nine string guitar so that Ken could play bass with just two fingers," Terry recalls. "The high end was like a twelve string with octaves, while the low end was like a regular six string guitar." The intent was to try and fill out the sound. The four of them took a dingy apartment on Huron Street. "I had the only alarm clock," Ken remembers, "and I would wake everybody else up and cook them breakfast. Then we would go and practice for the day and come back and I would cook us dinner." Scott Young arranged for the band to practice in the lobby of the Poor Alex Theater, an old establishment on Bloor Street in downtown Toronto. He also paid the theater rental for them until they could get on their feet. This was an about-face for the man who had stubbornly refused to support his son's musical career in the past. Scott even co-signed a $400 loan for Neil to provide him with survival money while the band rehearsed. It was to be repaid at a later date. These incidents signaled a begrudging acceptance of Neil's chosen vocation, at least temporarily. The band used the tiny theater by day, vacating it in the evening to allow movies to be shown.

Soon after his arrival in Toronto, Neil had telephoned the manager of the Allen Ward Trio, Martin Onrot. "Craig Allen had told me that a rock group they had met in Fort William might be coming to see me," recalls Martin. "I said, 'A rock group?!' and Craig said they were doing rock and folk music together and were really good." Martin had been on the local folk scene for a few years having been involved with the Mariposa Folk Festival and had managed the Fifth Peg folk club on Church Street. Always on the lookout for new talent, he agreed to audition the band. "They were doing a fair amount of original material," he says, "Neil's stuff, and that's what attracted me to them. They were so far ahead of where music was or where it was going. Neil had such a unique style and a unique voice." Martin came up with the idea of naming the quartet 4 To Go. "It was a cute play on words but I don't think that any of them were particularly fond of that name." For a time, the group referred to themselves as The Castaways, after Ken's cast.

During those early weeks in Toronto, Neil had not forgotten about Mort the hearse. Frequent phone calls were made to Bill's Garage in Blind River to find out if a replacement transmission had been located. That was no easy task for a 1948 Buick Roadmaster hearse. Neil and Terry returned to Blind River by bus on two or three occasions believing that the vehicle was repaired. Each time they came back disappointed. On the last trip to the garage, Bill assured them that a replacement had indeed been found. "My mother sent me some money for the new transmission, so Terry and I went back and they put it in. We got out on the road and I was ecstatic. Then that sound started again. Something was wrong with the rear end. So eventually I just left it there for good. It was really hard for me to let it go. I loved that hearse." A decade later, Neil lamented the loss of his hearse in the song *Long May You Run* on the 1976 STILLS-YOUNG BAND album.

While Martin made the rounds of the clubs and coffeehouses trying to sell 4 To Go, once again Neil's revolving door of sidemen swung around. Bob Clark was the first "one to go." In a perpetual state of poverty, Bob's mother had sent him $20.00. Despite their shared condition, Bob spent the money on a record album, a movie and popcorn. "We were so intense in those days," affirms Neil. "When I would get money from people, that money didn't go towards parties or clothes. It only went towards getting to the next musical place or trying to make things happen with the band. I was really into it." The final straw came when Martin suggested they enhance their sound by working on four part harmony singing. Tight harmonies were a highlight of the Allen Ward Trio's folk sound, and Neil liked that group. Neil, Ken, and Terry were game but Bob balked. He was a drummer, he insisted, not a singer. In a letter to Diana Halter back in Winnipeg that summer, Ken hinted of the impending change when he told her that Bob was unhappy over having to sing. "I think we're going to be looking for a new drummer," he wrote. Soon after, Bob Clark was out.

Bob drifted back to Winnipeg where he filled the drum stool for his brother at Chan's Moon Room for awhile but it wasn't his kind of music. Returning to Toronto, he ended up at Scott's house a couple of times for a meal and a place to sleep. "Scott kind of looked after him," recalls Liz Clark. "He was very good to Bob and all those boys." Bob eventually joined The Marquis, a Niagara Falls based Top 40 bar band, with whom he recorded two singles, *Put the Torch To Me* for the Melbourne label in 1968 and *Rockin' Crickets* for Canadian Artists Records in 1969. Not long after that last recording, Bob was killed in a freak highway accident near Halifax, Nova Scotia. The car he was driving, a Mustang he had just purchased, missed a turn on a winding stretch of highway. Rolling off the pavement, the car hit some rocks and burst into flames. Bob Clark was barely twenty-two years old. It would be years later before Neil learned of his friend's death.

Terry Erickson was the next to depart. With prospects for employment for 4 To Go looking slim, he resurrected his earlier plan to go to England. "We were starving and there wasn't anything happening workwise for us so I phoned an agent in Liverpool and lined up some gigs. But for some reason Neil didn't want to go, so I phoned back and asked if I could do them as a single and they said okay." Neil later explained the reason. "I didn't want to go to England by then. I wanted to go to California. That was where the sounds I was hearing were coming from." Terry made the journey overseas and played around Liverpool for eight months as both a solo act and with a local group called Them Grimbles. Returning to Thunder Bay, he later joined the Canadian Armed Forces. He offers this assessment of Neil at that time. "Music was the most important thing in Neil's life. He wanted to make music his life and he wanted success out of it but at the time we were together in Toronto, he didn't know which way to go. He eventually realized that you couldn't do anything in this country unless you left."

New recruits were required. The first to join was Jim Ackroyd, a former Winnipegger who had relocated to Toronto a year earlier. Jim had been a member of The Galaxies, an influential band on the early Winnipeg community club scene and favorites of radio station CKRC. He and Ken Koblun had both grown up in the Fort Rouge district. The Squires and The Galaxies had often crossed paths on the same Winnipeg gig circuit. As a guitarist and bass player with a blossoming enthusiasm for folk music, he later led the folk-bluegrass outfit James and the Good Brothers in Toronto. Ackroyd was the perfect replacement for Terry. In fact, it was Terry who found Jim for the band. "Jimmy and I had been friends as kids in Kenora, Ontario," Terry relates. "He was playing with a group at the Purple Onion so I told him that I was leaving Neil and he was interested in joining them." As Jim recalls, "Neil and I and Ken knew each other from Winnipeg and we were living down the street from each other on Huron Street in Yorkville. They were doing a lot of Neil's own songs and Neil and I wrote a song together, though I can't remember what it was now." Ken recalls one song Neil wrote at that time, *Casting Me Away From You*. Although never recorded, the song surfaced in a different form years later. "That song was later the basis for the instrumental *The Emperor of Wyoming* on his first solo album," offers Ken. "He must have not liked the words or forgotten them but he kept the melody. *Girl in the Mirror* might have been started in Toronto finished it in Los Angeles with the Springfield."

sulting the bulletin board at Long and McQuade
on Bloor Street, Neil found a drummer. Musicians
between ds or seeking to launch themselves onto the music
scene would post their name and phone number on the board. A
similar practice had existed at Winnipeg Piano where Neil used to
hang out. Geordie McDonald had placed his name on the back of
another musician's card at the store and Neil called him. It was by
now September of 1965. "I had been playing music for about five
years," states Geordie, "and was a graduate of Oscar Peterson's
School of Music. I was just looking for a gig and was willing to try
rock music. I went over to a studio near Yonge and Bloor, Bianca
Robe's dance studio, where I auditioned for Neil. I had to change
my style to fit the group because I had never played that kind of
music before. He played me some of his songs and said, 'This is
what we're doing and it's called folk rock.' I asked Neil if what I
was playing was appropriate. All he said was, 'That's okay.'" With
this new lineup, the band returned to the Poor Alex again to practice for their assault on Toronto's ears.

During this time, Neil had moved from Huron Street to an
apartment on St. George Avenue. He later moved into Geordie's
apartment at 88 Isabella near Yorkville village, a house he memori-
alized in the song *Ambulance Blues* on his ON THE BEACH album:

Oh Isabella, proud Isabella.
They tore you down,
And plowed you under.

AMBULANCE BLUES, 1974

To earn a living while 4 To Go rehearsed, Geordie had secured a gig
with a jazz group, and while away in Montreal for a week, offered
the pad to Neil who moved in and eventually stayed. Geordie
found another apartment. He recalls a humorous moment. "I had
an evening gig with the jazz group at the Waldorf Astoria in downtown Toronto. It was sort of a classy place. Neil came by to see me
one night and they kicked him out because he had long hair."

The band followed a strict rehearsal schedule each day,

enforced by Neil. He was firmly in control. "Neil seemed to be natural leader who knew exactly what he wanted," states Geordie. "He was very intense and highly focused. When things went wrong he would throw a Coke bottle across the room. But I never had any problems with Neil because I was a very serious musician too. We worked on his tunes, though I also recall doing Dylan's *Just Like Tom Thumb's Blues*. But he was always writing songs."

Martin Onrot, meanwhile, was facing stonewalls wherever he turned. He brought record producers and club owners down to the Poor Alex but could not secure the band a gig. "The club owners and record people had a closet mentality," he recalls. "They were looking for a very prescribed rock 'n' roll sound and didn't want anything original. Originality was difficult to sell and Neil was an original. Bands like The Paupers and The Mandala were unique at that time but most of the bands playing around town were just rock 'n' roll bands. All the icons were American and British groups and everything had to appeal to people that way. Neil's music couldn't be pigeonholed and unfortunately that was what people wanted." Neil had given Martin copies of the Fort William recordings to hustle to record companies. Martin even made the rounds of companies in New York but to no avail.

"Toronto was so negative," states Onrot. "It just wasn't happening for Neil. We were sitting one night in my car outside his apartment on Isabella and he was so very unhappy that he couldn't get any attention. He was frustrated."

Neil's frustration with this lack of success later surfaced in the lyrics for his song *The Last Trip to Tulsa* on his first solo album, NEIL YOUNG:

> *I used to be folksinger keeping managers alive,*
> *When you saw me on a corner and told me I was jive,*
> *So I unlocked your mind to see what I could see,*
> *If you guarantee the postage, I'll mail you back the key.*

THE LAST TRIP TO TULSA, 1968

In order to repay his father for the loan secured that summer, Neil took a job as a stock boy at a Coles bookstore at the corner of Yonge

N'T BE DENIED

ıe in downtown Toronto, not far from the village.
.air cut to a respectable length for the interview.
...s entry into the workaday world lasted a short five
.. Neil was frequently absent or late and the manager at Coles
ıet him go. Staying up all night making music with friends in the village cramped his day job. That short-lived experience at Coles remains Neil's one and only excursion into a normal employment routine. He has always made his way in life through music.

By late September the writing was on the wall. Four To Go had come and gone without ever playing an engagement. "We sort of died out in Toronto," reflects Neil. "We sort of lost our spirit. All we did was practice. We never had a gig. All the time I was in Toronto, I never played one of my own songs with a band to an audience. I think the problem was that people were telling us what to do, what to sound like, rather than the cool thing we had happening in Fort William. Toronto was all locked up." The experience was disheartening and disillusioning. But it did not dampen Neil's determination to stick with his vision. If Toronto didn't want Neil Young the folk rock band leader, then they might want Neil Young the solo folk singer.

Neil returned to Yorkville in February 1969, performing songs from his first solo album at the Riverboat Coffee House.

RIVERBOAT

COFFEE HOUSE

134 YORKVILLE AVE. 922-6216

EVERY NIGHT
(EXCEPT MONDAY)
8 p.m. - 3 a.m.

The Riverboat re-opens Jan. 6 with an important new composer
and folksinger that everyone is talking about . . .

Maurey Haydn

JAN.
14-26
BUDDY GUY
CHICAGO BLUES BAND
Brilliant guitarist, outstanding blues vocalist

JAN. 28-FEB. 2
MIKE SEEGER

FEB.
4-9
NEIL YOUNG
former lead guitarist, singer, composer with
THE BUFFALO SPRINGFIELD

FEB. 11-16
DOC WATSON

FEB. 18-23
JOHN HAMMOND
His voice is a supple multi-coloured instrument capturing the
tension, rhythmic drive and emotional anguish of the deep blues . .
Robert Sheldon, New York Times

SPIDER JOHN KOERNER
FEB. 25 – MARCH 2

JERRY JEFF WALKER
MARCH 4-9
Hit single and album Mr. BOJANGLES

Lenny Breau
master guitarist jams the Riverboat every time.
MARCH 11-16

RIVERBOAT presents at MASSEY HALL
ORDON LIGHTFOOT
MARCH
29, 30, 31

*Neil's father, Scott
Young, joined him
backstage at the
Riverboat.*

Neil joined Ricky James Matthews (Rick James) and the Mynah Birds to perform in Toronto and to record in Detroit for Motown Records. The Mynah Birds are shown here with Matthews (James) on lead vocals and tambourine but without Young.

Neil returned to Toronto again in 1971 to play two sold-out concerts at Massey Hall on his "Journey Thru the Past" tour.

Neil greeted old friends and family members backstage at this impromtu homecoming party.

During this time, Neil's image (over) first appeared in Rolling Stone magazine.

NINE

NOWADAYS CLANCY CAN'T EVEN SING

Hey, who's that stomping all over my face?
Where's that silhouette I'm trying to trace?
Who's that putting sponge in the bells
  I once rung?
And taken my gypsy before she's begun?

Nowadays Clancy Can't Even Sing, 1965

With his electric folk rock vision temporarily on hold, Neil prowled the streets of Yorkville village, meeting musicians and "scene-makers," frequenting more coffeehouses than rock 'n' roll bars. He was listening to the sounds of Yorkville, and these sounds were influencing him and his writing. The frustration he was facing just trying to get a band going manifested itself in the songs he began to write. The autumn and early winter of 1965 were Neil's blue period, a time of reflection on what he was doing and where he wanted to go. His lyrics turned more introspective, deeper, moodier. In marked contrast to the trend at the time of folkies turning electric and joining bands, Neil was beginning to consider abandoning rock bands for a solo career as a singer-song-writer. "Neil had been on his own for a month after the band broke up," Ken Koblun remembers, "and he was getting really depressed. He started writing all these serious songs."

Out of this period came songs like *The Rent Is Always Due*, *Don't Pity Me Babe*, and *Extra Extra*. All revealed Young's growing fascination with Dylan's oblique lyricism, as well as his disillusion-ment with his current predicament:

Who says you're coming on,
Don't think you're living long
They won't remember you,
The rent is always due.

He later resurrected part of the chord progression from this song for his 1968 Buffalo Springfield classic, *I Am a Child*.

Extra Extra, sometimes mistakenly referred to as "When It Falls, It Falls All Over You," from the chorus lyrics, spells out his frustration at this time in his life. One can only speculate on the name of the "old man" personified in *Extra, Extra*, but Neil's sense of helplessness in face of the breakup of his family would seem to inspire this song, as it would the lyrics to *"Helpless"* later recorded with Crosby, Still, Nash & Young on the DEJA VU album. Neil was certainly in a reflective mood at this pivotal point in his career:

Selling papers on the corner,
I saw a man yesterday.
I asked him if he'd wanna,
Tell me what made him this way.
He said, "When it's born, it's warms,
Then it gathers strength and lies.
When it falls, it falls all over you."

He used to pick his friends,
They left him in the end,
An easy thing to lose,
The right to pick and choose.

He said he left his wife,
The backbone of his life.
Another came along,
But now I guess she's gone.

I think I used to see,
That old man on tv.
Can you be the same?
It seems like such a shame.
He said "When it's born, it's warm,
Then it gathers strength and lies.
When it falls, it falls all over you."

EXTRA, EXTRA, 1965

Although recorded later that fall in a demo session and as an early Buffalo Springfield recording, *Extra, Extra* has never been offered for public consumption.

But the composition that best captured Neil's mood that autumn was to become the song that would ultimately bring him his first taste of real success on a massive scale. *Nowadays Clancy Can't Even Sing* remains a masterpiece of alienation. It was born out of his frustration and hopelessness following the break up of his band and his failure to garner any interest for what he was trying to say musically:

Hey, who's that stomping all over my face?
Where's that silhouette I'm trying to trace?
Who's putting sponge in the bells I once rung?
And taken my gypsy before she's begun?

Who's saying, "Baby that don't mean a thing,"
Cause nowadays Clancy can't even sing.

Who's comin' home on old 95?
Who's got the feelin' to keep him alive?
Though having it, sharing it ain't quite the same.
It ain't a gold nugget, you can't lay a claim.
Who's saying, "Baby that don't mean a thing,"
Cause nowadays Clancy can't even sing.

NOWADAYS CLANCY CAN'T EVEN SING, 1965

The character is loosely based on someone Neil knew of back at
Kelvin High School, Clancy Smith. "He was a kind of persecuted
member of the community. He used to be able to do something,
sing or something, and then he wasn't able to do it anymore. The
fact was that all the other problems or things that were seemingly
important didn't mean anything anymore because he couldn't do
what he wanted to do." The theme is a metaphor for Neil's frustrations in Toronto.

Diana Halter sheds more light on the origins of the song.
"Clancy Smith went to Kelvin when Neil did. I've known him for
years. He was stricken with multiple sclerosis. *Nowadays Clancy
Can't Even Sing* was kind of about him but was more or less written
about the awkwardness of people who don't fit into the status
quo. Clancy personified the person that you couldn't get into
because he was so intelligent and so bright that he masked the
sweet soul beneath it all. He was awkward with people. I think
Neil saw this as being a great handicap. The whole thing of the
sixties was having to be a part of the status quo and Clancy was
very isolated in his social capacities. I think Neil broke through a
few times and saw him as the person who personified intense people

who can't express themselves. That whole song is about how difficult it is to fit in. Neil saw a poignancy in his geekiness. He was quite a character, but he always shrugged off the notion that the song was about him." Neil and Clancy both attended the Kelvin High School reunion in 1987. "I brought Neil over to see Clancy," says Diana, "and they talked for some time. That was an interesting reunion, Neil and Clancy!" Although the personification of Clancy Smith's frustration and Neil's inability to gain momentum in his career remain in the chorus throughout the song, Neil has suggested in later interviews that the song also deals with his feelings over the breakup of a relationship with an old girlfriend. Again, like the best of his material, Neil draws inspiration from a variety of personal recollections and inspirations. Like Dylan, Neil's lyrics are never easily interpreted.

That fall, Neil paid a short visit home to see his mother. The trip by train may have influenced the line in Clancy about coming home on old 95. Marilyn Borden, a first year university student from River Heights, met Neil at a party in St. Vital while he was home. "We hung out together for those two weeks," she recalls, "though my parents didn't approve because to them, he was a just high school dropout." She recalls their time together. "He had a one-track mind. All he talked about was music and about going back down east. He talked about going to New York as well." Marilyn saw Neil perform solo at the 4-D. "Afterwards, we went over to Bill Edmundson's apartment where the two of them worked on songs together. He wrote a song for me and gave me the lyrics. It was called *Our Time*, and had the line, "The fading mist of your perfume," chuckles Marilyn. "I think I started writing *The Rent Is Always Due* when I was back in Winnipeg," speculates Neil. Soon after, he was back on the train, ready to give Toronto another try.

While Neil was brooding on his own, Ken Koblun set about establishing himself as an itinerant bass player on the Yorkville folk scene. "While my hand had been healing, Martin Onrot had taken me down to the Riverboat and introduced me to Bernie Fiedler," Koblun recalls. "Bernie eventually gave me a job washing dishes and handing out advertising handbills. Then I started working at the club backing up folk singers." Geordie McDonald continued to do jazz and nightclub gigs in and around Toronto. Jim Ackroyd formed a group first called The Knack then later The Dickens and set off to work the New England college circuit. Despite the lean times, Neil kept in touch with Ken and Geordie. Like most musicians in Toronto, their paths often crossed in the village. "Neil and I would hang out together once in awhile," recalls Geordie. "I remember playing him a lot of strange records, avant garde stuff like Sun Ra. I was into that kind of stuff. He listened to it, he was a very open person, but he said it didn't relate to what he wanted to do." He recalls a humorous incident. "We went down to the River- boat one night to see Jesse Colin Young. I knew the drummer and Neil had met Jesse in a coffeehouse. He invited us to come down and sit in with him but the guy at the door would not let us in. Koblun was inside handing out handbills but he couldn't get us inside either." The two plotted their revenge on the club. Neil's depressed state had not dampened his wry sense of humor. A few days later a rumor of an impromptu visit to the club by Bob Dylan was circulating through the village. Neil and Geordie saw their chance. "Neil and I phoned the club and I put on a Bob Dylan impression and said I was dropping by in ten minutes. The people in the club stayed up until about six in the morning waiting for Dylan to show but he never did. Neil loved that."

After the band had been apart for a month or so, Geordie sug- gested they take a gig in Vermont. Jim Ackroyd was out of the pic- ture by then, but Neil and Ken jumped at the opportunity. The pre- vious year, Geordie had done a gig at a ski resort in Killington, Vermont. He called the resort, the Wobbly Barn, to arrange an audi- tion for the group. If it went well, the manager assured them, they had the gig for the entire winter season. It was October 30, the day before Hallowe'en, when the band traveled by bus to Vermont. In the Buffalo bus station, the trio posed for a quick picture at a photo booth. Geordie vividly recalls Neil writing songs on the bus with a little flashlight. He had completed writing *Clancy* prior to the trip. But the Vermont gig proved a disaster. "It was a really lame gig," states Neil. "We only played one night. We weren't what they want- ed and they didn't like us." Geordie adds, "Neil felt like leaving and he was right because the owner was an idiot. He asked us if we played La Bamba. I said no and the guy said, 'In that case forget it.'" During the evening a drunk accidently broke one of Neil's guitar strings and that was it for him. "I tried to get Neil to stay but he said he didn't want to play bars. He said, 'I don't like this scene, I'm going to New York.'" That was the last time Geordie saw Neil. Later, back in Toronto, Geordie and Ken tried to find a guitarist to complete the Vermont engagement but were unsuccessful.

While Geordie returned to Toronto, Neil was again off on another impetuous adventure. This time he did not leave Ken behind. "Neil and I said, 'Let's go visit Jean Gurney in New York.' She was the girl singer from The Company that I had been corresponding with since Fort William. So we called her and she said, 'Come on down.'" The two, along with all their guitars and amplifiers, took the bus to New York. "We carried our equipment from the bus depot through Grand Central Station to a cab," recalls Ken. "No one would help us. One cabbie just said, 'Hey kid, you're in the Big Apple now, lug it yourself.'"

While Ken visited with his lady friend, Neil went in search of his old Fort William buddy, Stephen Stills. He assumed that Stephen had returned to New York following The Company's Canadian tour. Armed with an address from that meeting six months earlier, Neil arrived at 171 Thompson Street, only to find Stephen's roommate, Richie Furay. Richie informed him that Stephen had left New York for California months earlier. Richie had chosen to remain in New York. "I met Richie and played him some of my songs and taught him *Clancy*," recalls Neil. Richie relates their meeting: "After the Au Go Go Singers broke up, I was working at Pratt and Whitney Aircraft in Connecticut and I maintained or helped keep an apartment with some of the Au Go Go Singers in New York. Stephen had told Neil earlier to go by that apartment if he was ever in New York. So Neil stopped by the apartment while I was there, down from Connecticut, and he taught me *Nowadays Clancy Can't Even Sing*. I thought it was a real fantastic song. I remember thinking, 'This guy's a pretty interesting guy.'" Richie goes on to describe the unique appeal that *Clancy* had. "It had a haunting melody to me, maybe it was the way Neil sang it. It was certainly not a typical song like the kind I was used to listening to. The song was really unique. It had metaphors and allegories about this classmate named Clancy who was just one of those guys everybody picked on." And his impression of Neil? "Neil seemed very sure of himself, of where he was going and was very intense. He impressed me so much as an artist and song-writer." Richie had Neil record the song on his tape recorder and write out the lyrics for him. Richie even performed the song at a couple of auditions he attended as a solo singer at the Bitter End folk club. Neil and Ken remained in New York for three days before returning by bus to Toronto. The trip had been an interest-ing diversion from the frustrations back in Canada and, although Neil went north, his song *Clancy* would shortly travel south to California. Unbeknownst to Neil, the seeds of future success were planted on that impulsive excursion.

Upon their return, the two friends parted company. Ken had lined up a gig with folksingers Jim and Jean, and promptly left for a tour of Massachusetts, New York, and Montreal. That tour brought him to the legendary Cafe Au Go Go in Greenwich Vil-lage in November. Meanwhile, Neil hung around Yorkville, crash-ing wherever he could find a spare bed. He had made the decision to pursue a solo folk singer direction but he still lacked a gig. Act-ing out of necessity, Neil's next move was one that he later regret-ted. "I sold my orange Gretsch electric guitar to get an acoustic twelve string. It was a stupid move but I needed the money. I had switched to become a singer/songwriter and that was the kind of guitar I needed because I was going folk music." When Rassy heard what he had done she was furious. "He had that beautiful guitar that I bought him with the white case that had been signed by everyone he had worked with or met, even Stephen Stills."

Through sheer tenacity, Neil secured a few solo engagements. "I had more success doing that in Yorkville than playing in groups," he states. "I actually did some coffeehouse gigs by myself in Yorkville. I played the Bohemian Embassy and another club called The New Gate of Cleve." For his solo folk gigs, Neil per-formed a mixture of personal favorites from other repertoires, including those of Bob Dylan, Phil Ochs, and Hamilton Camp, and his own material, much of it written recently while scuffling in Toronto. He even performed *Sugar Mountain*, his Fort William lament to growing out of his teens, a song he had never done with his bands. Hunched over his guitar, eyes closed, Neil's intense presence on the tiny coffeehouse stages created an intimate and personal experience. As he performed each song he was transported to another plane, like that feeling he experienced one night at the Flamingo Club in Fort William when he first found himself transcending consciousness while playing *Farmer John*. This time there was no electric band to support him and no amplified volume to pump up the excitement, just Neil, his songs, and the audience. He had witnessed enough folk performances to know that it's the songs, the lyrics, that create the mood more than the performance. Neil's songs were stripped to their basics, revealing the bare emotion, frustration, and yearning he was feeling then. He would introduce each song, offering the audience a brief glimpse of the motivation behind them. But his between song chat was minimal, the songs had to stand on their own. For Neil it was essential that people listen to what he had to say. He would become irritated when audience-members talked or walked in or out of the room during his performance. His songs were a dialogue between him and the audience, an intensely personal experience. The fact that not enough people did listen or appreciate him was a further source of frustration. A review of one of his folk engagements in December of 1965 was not encouraging. "My folk singing career didn't really go over very well in Toronto," offers Neil. "There was a review of one of my shows in a newspaper and it said my songs were all like a cliché." His sense of rejection, if not pain, surfaced in the lyrics for *Ambulance Blues* some years later:

> *Well I'm up in TO keepin' jive alive,*
> *And out on the corner it's half past five.*
> *But the subways are empty,*
> *And so are the cars,*
> *Except for the Farmer's Market.*
> *And I still can hear him sayin',*
> *"You're all just pissin' in the wind.*
> *You don't know it but you are."*

AMBULANCE BLUES, 1974

Wounded but still in the game, Neil continued writing, hustling for folk gigs anywhere. He became a fixture on the folk scene, more as someone everybody knew than ever saw performing. Bruce Palmer, another village habitué, recalls that Neil would play with anyone back then and had earned a begrudging respect from the folk community for his determination, if less so for his talent. Neil ran into Joni Mitchell on occasion in the village. They remembered each other from the year before at the 4-D coffeehouse in Winnipeg. Joni was in the process of leaving her husband and singing partner Chuck. She was now working solo, and she was talking of striking out for New York to try her luck in Greenwich Village. On one occasion that winter, Neil and Martin Onrot drove down to Detroit to visit Joni.

Neil paid another brief visit to New York in November. A demo recording session had been arranged at Elektra Records studio and Neil flew in and out of the Big Apple. He remains unsure of who actually secured this session, but it was not Martin Onrot. Although Neil was still legally signed exclusively to Martin, the manager had been forced to abandon Neil due to the general lack of interest in him. Martin had not, however, lost faith in Neil's talent. He just couldn't sell him. Regardless, the session was not what Neil had expected. "I thought I was going to record in their studio. I saw when I came in that Judy Collins was in the studio and they were doing one of her songs that later became well known. They had the track and I could hear them working on it. I thought, 'This is great, I'm in a real recording studio now!' Then we turned right and went through a door and there were all these tapes all over the shelves. I was in the tape library. This guy brings in this funky old tape recorder and puts it on a metal chair and says, 'Just sing 'em all into this, it'll be fine.' I didn't feel very good about what I was doing."

Shaken, Neil hastily played seven songs, all, with the exception of *Sugar Mountain*, written while in Toronto. The tape reveals a nervous young man, fumbling with his guitar tuning, performing his songs in a rushed manner as if intimidated by his surroundings. The session marked the one and only time that Neil has sung *Clancy* on an official recording session. It was also the

recording debut of *Sugar Mountain*, a song Neil wc
shelve until his post-Springfield solo career in 1?
included *Don't Pity Me Babe*, a loose derivative of tnc
song, *I Wonder*, appearing ten years later as *Don't Cry No Tears*
his ZUMA album. A reference to Peggy in the song is explained
thusly by Neil: "It was a fictitious name I used based on a part of
the guitar. Peggy Grover was Grover pegs, the brand of tuning
pegs on a guitar."

> *Young Peggy just died today.*
> *Young Peggy just died today.*
> *I guess nobody even knows the case,*
> *But the way the story goes,*
> *She just ran out of clothes*
> *No will, this world just wore the Peg down.*
> *Last words, can't talk, and then she wrote.*
>
> *Don't see no tears around me.*
> *Don't see no tears around me.*
> *I don't take much stock,*
> *In the things people say.*
> *I'm not saying that they're wrong,*
> *They've just been standing around too long.*
> *Gone bad, oh no don't pity me babe,*
> *I know I'm alright.*
> *Oh yeah, I'm alright.*

> *DON'T PITY ME BABE*, 1965

Extra, Extra made its debut as well. Rounding out the session were
I Ain't Got The Blues, The Rent Is Always Due, and *Run Around Babe*.
These latter are rather undistinguished songs. Indeed, the entire
session revealed nothing of the major talent that Neil possessed
and merely provide the listener with a moment in history rather
than an historic performance. Little came of this session. It seems
that Elektra was as disinterested in Neil Young's songs as Toronto
audiences were.

Meanwhile, Ken Koblun's fortunes had been faring much better than Neil's. After his stint with Jim and Jean, he found himself in demand on the growing folk rock scene. At various times he worked with The Dirty Shames, David Blue, his old friends the Allen Ward Trio, Carolyn Hester, The Stormy Clovers, and Vicki Taylor. In early 1966, Koblun joined promising folk rockers Three's A Crowd. Formed in Vancouver as a kind of Canuck version of Peter, Paul and Mary, the group had migrated to Toronto and become a major attraction in the coffeehouses. By the time Ken joined, the group were regulars at the prestigious Riverboat, an ironic twist of fate for Ken whose previous job there was as a dish washer. By bringing in Ken on bass and drummer Richard Patterson, formerly of Ottawa's very own Esquires (another twist of fate for Koblun), Three's A Crowd were beginning to bridge the folk-rock gap successfully. Their unique sound and comic stage antics drew the attention of The Mamas and the Papas' rotund singer Mama Cass Elliot. She produced their one and only album in 1967, CHRISTOPHER'S MOVIE MATINEE, which featured Ken's fine bass playing and boasted four songs by then up-and-coming singer/songwriter Bruce Cockburn and one by Yorkville's Murray McLauchlan. The album typified the Yorkville folk-rock sound at that time and was well received. They toured Canada and the northern U.S.A. They went on to become featured performers for Canada's centennial birthday celebrations at Montreal's Expo 67.

In the cold, damp days of January 1966, Neil continued his transient life in Yorkville. For a time he lived above a coffeehouse on Avenue Road. He was sometimes in the company of a young folksinger friend named Tannis Neiman. He saw his father infrequently, stopping by for a meal. On one particularly cold day, Scott found Neil wandering down Yonge without gloves on his hands. Scott stopped and offered to buy him a pair, but Neil refused and carried on, preoccupied. Music was never far from his mind. In his 1973 song *Time Fades Away*, he alludes to this period when he sings:

Back in Canada I spent my days
Riding subways through a haze.
I was handcuffed, I was born and raised.
Son, don't be home too late,
Try to get back by eight.
Son, don't wait til the break of day,
Cause you know how time fades away.

TIME FADES AWAY, 1973

He wrote to his mother that early winter and mentioned a possible recording session in Toronto with Ken Koblun and David Rae, the talented guitar player with the Allen Ward Trio but, typically, nothing came of it. It was around this time that Neil met Bruce Palmer. Bruce had earned a name for himself with Jack London and the Sparrow, a well respected Toronto group. Just nineteen, he already had plenty of experience in music and in being on his own. He and Neil had much in common and struck up a friendship after a chance encounter in the village. "I ran into Neil on Yorkville Avenue," recalls Bruce. "He was carrying an amplifier head on his head. You didn't see many people carrying that around back then. He was looking for people to play music with, so I asked him to join my group."

With prospects for his singer/songwriter career no better than they were before Christmas, Neil was in desperate need of a new plan. Bruce offered it. He was in a band called The Mynah Birds and their guitar player had just quit. "Our manager owned a Mynah bird store where he actually sold Mynah birds. We were more of an attraction for him to sell more birds," laughs Bruce. "He dressed us up in yellow boots, black leather jackets, and yellow turtlenecks so we looked like Mynah birds. That was the group before Neil joined. This guy also owned the Mynah Bird club which offered the first body painting in Toronto. A girl sat in a bikini and people painted her with finger paints. He was a real entrepreneur!" Prior to Neil's entrance into the band, The Mynah Birds had recorded a song for Columbia Records in Canada, *Mynah Bird Hop*. Bruce's offer to Neil was a surprising move considering that Neil had foresaken electric rock for acoustic twelve string folk. "It was the most ridiculous thing ever heard of," offers Bruce, regarding Neil's use of a folk guitar in a rock 'n' roll group. "I don't know why we even considered that instrument but we did and it worked."

The offer came at the right time for Neil. "I had to eat. I needed a job and it seemed like a good thing to do. I still liked playing and I liked Bruce so I went along. There was no pressure on me. It was the first time that I was in a band where I wasn't calling the shots." The star attraction for The Mynah Birds was not Neil but singer Ricky James Matthews, a self-styled black Mick Jagger. When Matthews' rhythm and blues vocals combined with Neil's twelve string acoustic sound, the band was an instant attraction, if for nothing other than curiosity. By combining these two potent formulas, The Mynah Birds were bridging the two Toronto styles, Yorkville and Yonge Street. By 1966, rock 'n' roll was beginning to supplant folk music as the staple fare in the Yorkville coffeehouses. The Purple Onion became the home for Luke and the Apostles, while Dee and the Yeoman held court at the Night Owl. A year later, Club 888, in the old Masonic Hall in the village, was converted into the legendary Rockpile. Jay Telfer, of the Toronto rock group A Passing Fancy, was around Yorkville at that time and witnessed a Mynah Birds performance. "Ricky James Matthews was a magical performer, a powerful singer and dynamic showman," he recalls. "He used to turn around and yell at Neil if he dropped his pick. Neil was playing so hard his fingers were bleeding." Neil reflects, "It was a good band. It had something going on. It was a folk rock kind of thing at first when I came along but then later it was just rock. They weren't doing any of my songs. It was more of a Rolling Stones kind of R 'n' B thing." Besides Neil, Bruce, and Ricky, the band also included John Yachimak on rhythm guitar and Ritchie Grand on drums.

The Mynah Birds' future looked even brighter when millionaire retailer John Craig Eaton took an interest in their music. As a member of the wealthy Eaton family, owners of the largest retail department store chain in Canada at that time, Eaton offered his financial assistance to further the group's career. For Neil, this meant new electric equipment. "I played a twelve string acoustic with a pickup at first but then I got a new six string Rickenbacker guitar from Eaton. When I came into the band, Eaton had already bought them a bunch of stuff like Traynor amplifiers. They were real good amps." For Eaton, his involvement with the band was recreational. "He would come down to the Patio Club," laughs Bruce, "and he would be like Knute Rockne, walking back and forth in his trenchcoat, as if he was a football coach addressing his team, saying 'Go get 'em guys!' Obviously it was a hobby for the man." Neil's sideman status was shortlived, however. "Rick and I started writing some songs together. And we recorded some of those songs. One song we wrote was called *It's My Time*. It was good, too."

Not only did joining The Mynah Birds keep Neil from starvation, it also opened up a whole new world hitherto unknown to him. "Ricky introduced me to amphetamines and that changed my life. When I had arrived in Toronto, there was a whole new culture that I was introduced to. I had done nothing like that up to then. Completely 'au natural.'" Fans of The Mynah Birds enjoyed the exuberance the musicians exhibited during performances. According to Neil, that exuberance was chemically induced. "We used to pop amyl nitrates before going on stage and walk on just killing ourselves laughing and rolling around from these things. We used to do all kinds of weird stuff. It was quite a time. I remember at a high-school gig, I was so high that I jumped off the stage and pulled my guitar jack out in the middle of a song."

With the right backing, The Mynah Birds were able to circumvent the traditional path to a recording contract, years of slugging it out in bars and on the road. Signed to Detroit's Motown label, the future looked rosy. Despite the presence of Ricky, the band was the first "white act" to sign with North America's premier black label. Each member signed a long term contract with Motown. And the label gave them the full treatment in the studio.

"We recorded for five or six nights and they gave us whatever we needed," recalls Neil. "If one of the guys couldn't play something, they just brought in one of their session players to do it. It was starting to sound hot." Bruce recalls that Smokey Robinson was involved, perhaps as producer. "He was in the studio a lot, walking around giving suggestions. I didn't even know what a producer did back then." Ken Koblun visited his old buddy during The Mynah Birds sessions in Detroit but was unimpressed. "There was no feel to that band, no drive. It just wasn't happening." No one will ever know. Disaster struck during the sessions. "We were just getting started," claims Neil, "when Ricky was busted. We knew he was an American but we didn't know he was a draft dodger." In fact, Ricky was AWOL from the U.S. Navy, no minor offense at the height of the Vietnam War. He surrendered to military authorities and served time in prison before eventually finding wealth and fame in the late 1970s as funk*meister* Rick James.

Motown suspended further recording sessions and, fortunately for Neil's later career, canceled The Mynah Birds' contract. The completed tapes, containing sixteen songs according to Bruce, were believed for years to have been lost by Motown during their move from Detroit to Los Angeles in the 1970s. However, a musicologist has recently stumbled upon them, mislabeled in Motown's vaults. A listen to the tapes reveals little sign of Neil's characteristic guitar or vocal. In fact, Neil did not sing on any of the recordings and his guitar playing is mixed down so low that it is virtually indistinguishable amid the other instruments. The only stand out feature is Ricky Matthews' voice.

The remaining band members limped back to Toronto. To add insult to injury, their manager had taken their Motown advance money and used it to score drugs and had overdosed, leaving them no singer and no money. The Mynah Birds died prematurely in early March 1966. In all, it had been a short rollercoaster ride. "The whole thing lasted only about six weeks," reflects Neil. "I only played a couple of gigs with The Mynah Birds before the recording sessions. I played a high school somewhere in Toronto and a couple of clubs like the Mynah Bird club, the El Patio, and Club 888 or something like that."

So once again Neil found himself without a band or a gig in Toronto. There was nothing for him in that city. "Toronto was a very humbling experience for me," cites Neil. "I just couldn't get anything going." It was time to move on. With the cool March wind blowing down Yonge Street, it took little to convince Neil that his next move should be south.

TEN

DOWN IN HOLLYWOOD

Oh Canada
We played all night.
I really hate to leave you now
But to stay just wouldn't be right.
Down in Hollywood
We played so good.
The businessmen crowded around
They came to hear the golden sound.
There we were on Sunset strip
Playing our songs for the highest bid.
We played all night
The price was right.

DON'T BE DENIED, 1973

"Canada just couldn't support the ideas I had. There wasn't a big enough audience for the music I wanted to do. I just couldn't get anyone to listen. There were some people who liked and supported what I was trying to do, there just weren't enough of them. By 1966, I knew I had to leave Canada, and the sounds I was hearing and the sounds I liked were coming from California. I knew that if I went down there I could take a shot at making it."

Today, the Canadian music industry is just that, an industry that brings in sales in the multi millions. Of the $250 million dollars earned through music product sales (cassettes, CDs and, to a much lesser extent now, albums), Canadian talent accounts for at least ten percent of that figure. That may not seem like much when compared to the American music industry where Michael Jackson's recording contract alone adds up to more than the total revenues of Canadian talent, but it is impressive when one considers the way it used to be in Canada. Prior to 1970, homegrown talent had a difficult uphill battle to earn attention in their own market. Canadian radio saturated listeners with American and British music, in some cases to the exclusion of the country's own musicians, singers, and songwriters. Put simply, the wisdom of the time was that a Canadian artist had not "made it" until he or she had achieved success south of the border.

This mindset made the fledgling Canadian recording industry in the early 1960s wary of artistic gambles. To be fair, there were many record companies here who signed Canadian artists and there were some national hits by Canadians such as The Guess Who's *Shakin' All Over* or records by Bobby Curtola, but generally record companies saw little revenue, and therefore not much incentive, in pushing Canadian acts. After all, despite the artistry and creativity of the music industry, it is still an industry and therefore is based on the bottom line. If it wasn't American or British, it stood little chance of reaching more than local ears.

Even the initial success of The Guess Who with *Shakin' All Over* was predicated on a slight of hand. Quality Records, their label in Canada, hearing a decidedly British sounding recording at a time when all things British sold, was reluctant to reveal the band's real Canuck identity on the label for fear of relegating the record to the garbage bin. So they concocted a clever plan to put

"Guess Who?" on the label and have people try to figure out which nifty, keen, gear, fab new British group of moptops was behind this sound. The deception worked, so well in fact that when the record took off across the country, Chad Allan and the Expressions received a phone call from Quality: "Guess what boys, your new name is Guess Who!" The industry philosophy was why tamper with a money maker. Needless to say, the band members hated the name. But as they say, money talks and bullshit walks; Chad Allan, Randy Bachman, and the others had suffered enough of the latter over the years to know the difference. Regrettably, once the word was out in the States that these boys were raised along the Red River rather than the Mersey, further releases died still-born over the next four years.

In order to combat the talent drain to the U.S., and in an attempt to keep at least some of the recording industry revenues in Canada, the government established Canadian content regulations for radio. "CanCon" rules require that radio stations in Canada play a minimum of 30 per cent Canadian recorded or produced records by Canadian artists. Initially a controversial move slammed by the radio industry, musicians in Canada hailed its implementation. What they saw was the chance to stagger the horse race in favor of Canadians and, in this way, give them the much needed exposure that would allow them to remain at home. The breakthrough successes internationally of Canadians like Gordon Lightfoot, Anne Murray, and The Guess Who, who returned to the charts with a string of million sellers in the early 1970s, only reinforced the benefits of CanCon. In fairness to the above-named artists whose stars had already risen before the regulations came into effect, what they did was to draw attention to the untapped talent still to be discovered in Canada. Surely, there were more Lightfoots, Murrays and Guess Whos in Canadian backyards — and there were.

The enormous international acclaim and vats of money Canadian rocker Bryan Adams has earned in the last ten years or so can be attributed to his talent and tenacity, and to CanCon. Though he is loathe to admit it, if it wasn't for CanCon, would he have ever been heard on Canadian radio when he first started out? Before CanCon, there were a lot of talented Canadians, many with the same potential as Adams, whose careers came and went without much opportunity to get their message to a wider audience. Many just quit trying and gave up. Others just gave up on Canada for the United States.

Neil Young had reached that conclusion after the demise of The Mynah Birds. That band had an opportunity few Canadian artists could claim and most envied at the time, an American recording contract. They had solid financial backing and, though only those few who were fortunate to witness their brief existence can attest, they had talent. But it all fell apart in the recording studio in Detroit. In retrospect, it seems unlikely, given the nature of Neil Young's career before that point and since, that he would have been happy for long in The Mynah Birds. It wasn't his band, he wasn't the leader, and they weren't doing his songs. Neil Young has always been a leader who charts his own course. Even in his later associations — the Buffalo Springfield, Crazy Horse, and Crosby, Stills, Nash & Young — Neil has been the loose cannon on deck, more prone to abandoning the ship than sticking through to the end of the voyage. As Stephen Stills maintains, Neil is not a team player.

By early 1966, Neil had given Toronto his best shot. He had tried it as leader of his own group, as a solo singer/songwriter, and as a member of someone else's band, all in vain. Most artists would have shrunk from this rejection and gone home to the ego-soothing reassurance of at least local acclaim. Not Neil. The determination that drove him in Winnipeg, through Fort William, and finally to Toronto, remained strong. He was not about to be denied. Still only twenty years old, Neil had proven that many times already. "I had to shit on a lot of people in one way or another and leave a lot of friends behind to get where I am now, especially in the beginning. There was no other way. I had almost no conscience for what I had to do. If I could justify it in terms of furthering my goal, I would just do it. And it's obvious when you look back at my early years, that's what I was like. I was so driven to make it."

Joni Mitchell was already attracting attention in New York's Greenwich Village. The Hawks had gone off with Dylan. The Sparrow were recording in New York. David Clayton Thomas was about to leave for that city, too. Across the border, Gordon Light-foot's name was appearing alongside Bob Dylan's name. He had even been signed up by Dylan's high profile New York-based manager, Albert Grossman. There was, for Neil, no other alternative. He felt he had to leave Toronto and Canada soon. "The most important thing for me back then was to keep moving so that I always had the advantage of being someone that people knew nothing about, the unknown factor."

Sitting in the Cellar coffeehouse on Yorkville Avenue in early March, Neil and Bruce Palmer tossed around ideas. They knew The Mynah Birds were finished but they also knew that they enjoyed playing together. Never fond of Canadian winters, not even the mild ones Toronto experiences, and aware that the style of music he sought was emanating from California, Neil convinced Bruce they had to go to Los Angeles. Besides the obvious attractions, Neil believed Stephen Stills was in Los Angeles at that moment and the opportunity to put something together with him was further inducement for heading south. Without hesitation, Bruce agreed. "We were like on a mission from God," reflects Neil, "and there was nothing going to stop us." Once again, Neil was acting on impulse, but unlike the ill-conceived Blind River excursion, this trip had a greater purpose. And Neil had an ally. "Bruce was there with me, determined to go," cites Neil. "He was as committed to go as I was." With the decision made, the only hurdle remained financing their expedition. The problem was the two had no money. Both had lived the transient life of a musician long enough to know that you kept few belongings besides what was necessary to play. Mobility was the key. They had little to sell to raise a road stake. In the end, they sold what little they possessed, and some things they didn't legally possess.

The latter turned out to be The Mynah Birds equipment. "Bruce and I pawned all the band's equipment," muses Neil. "It was the only way we could go. The band had broken up. Bruce and I were the only ones who wanted to be the band. Ricky was in jail. There was no Mynah Birds without him. It was the band's equipment but it was really Eaton's equipment." Gone was his new Rickenbacker guitar and Traynor amp and Bruce's amp, along with other sound equipment. That hasty action came back to haunt Neil years later. After he had become successful, he returned for an engagement at Massey Hall in Toronto in the early seventies. When John Craig Eaton heard of Neil's return, he had a court order impose a lien on Neil's wages from the concert, garnisheeing the amount owing for the Mynah Birds' gear five years earlier. "I paid the whole shot without question," states Neil. "I even paid for the other guys' equipment bought before I joined the band." In hindsight, it was a small price to pay when compared to the eventual dividends reaped by Neil as a result of that trip to California.

There was no time to lose. With the pawnshop money fresh in his hands, Neil checked the used car ads in the newspapers and scoured the car lots. He knew what he was looking for, and he soon found it — a 1953 Pontiac hearse. Word of the excursion had been passed among a few Yorkville friends who asked to come along for the adventure. It was almost like Blind River revisited. "We got the hearse and left within a couple of days,"Neil remembers. "We took one guy with us named Mike whose last name I can't remember, Tannis Neiman and another girl with long red hair, and a third girl, Jeannine. Three guys and three girls." It was mid March when the band of travelers, armed with guitars, a change of clothes, and plastic bags full of marijuana, bid farewell to Toronto and headed north on Highway 400.

North? Neil was no stranger to border crossings. Having lived in Winnipeg, a city only an hour from the U.S. border, he had crossed to the United States on occasion. As well, The Mynah Birds had crossed over to Detroit frequently during their brief recording career. He knew they would be hassled for certain if they crossed at Windsor-Detroit or Niagara Falls-Buffalo. Those customs posts were more used to turning away long haired teenagers. He recalled being told by musicians in Fort William that the U.S. customs office at Sault Ste. Marie on Lake Superior was a safe crossing, especially late at night. That would be their plan, but it required a detour of almost 700 kilometers. The others were not in favor of the extra distance, but Neil was in command of this voyage, so off they headed north and then west to Sault Ste. Marie. Ironically, the trip would take them past Bill's Garage in Blind River, though Neil declined to visit Mort.

The hearse, with its Bohemian occupants, arrived in Sault Ste.

Marie late at night after the first day of travel. "What we found at the border was laughable," offers Bruce. "There was this old man sitting in a rocking chair in front of a little shack out in the middle of nowhere." As is required, the American customs officer nervously approached the hearse. Scanning its motley crew amid the long hair, buckskin, and guitars, he asked the routine questions all Canadians are subjected to when crossing "the world's longest undefended border." Who are you, where are you coming from, are you Canadian citizens, and where are you going? Neil was ready for this. He knew what kind of reception they might expect to receive and that their chances of getting across were slim if they told the truth about their trip. "My Mom lives in Winnipeg and we're going to see her," was his confident reply to the last and most important question. Canadians traveling east to west or vice versa, frequently journey through the northern United States. Brandishing his Winnipeg address on a piece of identification as the icing on the cake, Neil offered a convincing tale. They were waved through. After a safe enough distance from the customs office, Neil found the turn off heading south and they were on their way.

They first headed due south to St. Louis, then west, via Route 66, to California; they were stopped frequently along the way by curious highway patrolmen. Route 66 had been immortalized in song first by torch singer Julie London and again in 1964 in a raunchy version by the Rolling Stones. "If you get hip to this kindly tip, and take that California trip. Get your kicks on Route 66," sneered the Stones' Mick Jagger. The highway had also been used as the title of a popular late 1950s television show that Neil had enjoyed, about two young men who set out in their red Corvette convertible in search of adventure. The significance of traveling down Route 66 was not lost on Neil.

In an ironic twist of fate, as the hearse rolled across the border and through the American Midwest in March en route to Los Angeles, Ken Koblun was on a plane leaving Los Angeles, where he had been visiting with Stephen Stills and Richie Furay, sounding out their offer to join a nascent band. When he and Neil had made that detour from Vermont to New York in early November of the previous year, they were looking for Stephen Stills. They had been disappointed to discover that he had departed to try his luck at getting something together in California. In Stephen's absence, Neil had met Richie Furay. It was at that meeting that Neil taught Richie his song *Clancy*. After Neil and Ken returned to Canada and scuffled about, Stephen convinced Richie to join him out in Los Angeles. "I was getting really frustrated with my job at Pratt and Whitney," states Richie. "It just wasn't the thing I wanted to do for the rest of my life, handing out tools. So I got in touch with Stephen by sending him a letter to the only address I had, his Dad's address in El Salvador. Somehow it got to his Mom in San Francisco and one way or another, it got to Stephen in Los Angeles. He sent a message back to me to get out there 'cause he had a group. But when I got there, the whole band was just him and me. It was frustrating but typical." In Los Angeles, Stephen had met Barry Friedman who encouraged him to get a group together. Friedman was on the periphery of the L.A. music scene and knew the right people in the business. Impressed with Stephen's songs and enthusiasm, he offered his assistance.

Prior to meeting Barry, Stephen had been attempting to launch himself on the Los Angeles music scene to general indifference. In an act of desperation that, fortunately for the music world, did not pan out, Stephen answered a casting call for young musicians to play the part of a fictitious rock group for a television show. The show turned out to be The Monkees. "I heard this open call go out around L.A.," Stephen recalls. "You didn't have to be a genius to figure out what happens to people that go on television. I figured what a great way to get a recording deal, write a bunch of songs, and make a bunch of money. So I went down and answered all their questions." Stephen possessed many of the requirements the producers were looking for: he sang, played guitar, and had youthful good looks with long blond hair. The problem was that he wanted to do his own songs. In their master plan to launch The Monkees onto the teenybop market, the producers had recruited a battery of the top songwriters in the business to provide ready-made material for the group. Who did this kid think he was, anyway? "When I asked the question about writing my own songs, they told me they had this publishing deal and had their writers already lined up. As it turned out, they didn't want me anyway, but I said, 'I have this friend,' and that was Peter Tork." Stephen's folkie friend from Greenwich Village, Peter Torkelson, auditioned and was accepted, with a quick alteration to his name. Stephen goes on to admit that if he had been chosen, he would have backed out of the Monkees deal anyway because he wanted to do his own material. He had been writing songs over the last year and possessed a keen ear for commerciality. Songs like *Neighbor Don't You Worry, Sit Down I Think I Love You,* and *Go And Say Goodbye,* written around that time, show Stephen's ease with phrases that offer lyrics in a straightforward, conversational manner between the writer and the listener. His style would later provide a potent contrast to Neil's more abstract word pictures on the Buffalo Springfield and CSN & Y recordings. The Monkees' loss was the music world's gain.

When Richie arrived in Los Angeles, he was dismayed to discover that Stephen had no band. Nevertheless, he decided to stick with Stephen. "We were living at Barry's house on Fountain Avenue, just hanging out learning each others' songs, trying to get a band together," recalls Richie. "A lot of the songs that Stephen sang on the first Buffalo Springfield album were already written by him then. Since we both had a mutual friend in Neil, I taught Stephen to play *Clancy.* We put it in our repertoire of songs." The two worked up a rock arrangement for the song and talked about what a band they could have if they could only find Neil. With Richie now on board, Stephen tried in vain to contact Neil to convince him to join them in L.A. But the only phone number he had was for Ken Koblun in Toronto. "Stephen Stills called me and told me that I should come down to California to join his band," recalls Ken. At the time, Ken was a member of Three's A Crowd who had just returned from a tour in western Canada that brought him back to play at Winnipeg's 4-D coffeehouse. He had lost touch with Neil by then but, like Richie, Ken took the bait and flew down to join Stephen's non-existent group. It was mid-March 1966.

A dubious Ken Koblun was reluctant to throw in his lot with the two singers. "Stephen and I thought we had convinced Ken to stay and be a part of our would-be group," recalls Richie. "We were all sleeping at Barry's house and we tried to bribe Ken to stay with a meal from Pioneer Chicken. We went to bed assured that he was going to stick around after the meal we bought him. I remember waking up in the morning and finding a note on the coffee table saying, 'Steve, I can't make it, sorry,' and he was gone. I don't know how he got away from us when we were all sleeping in the livingroom." Ken confirms the story. "I spent a week with Stills and Furay and nothing was happening. I had to make a decision. I had twenty dollars left in my pocket. Either spend it on food and stay with Stills in California, or spend it on taxi fare to L.A. airport and the manager from Three's A Crowd was going to pay for my ticket back to Toronto. So that was what I did."

So, while Ken was homeward bound having failed to get a group happening with Stephen, Neil was heading south in search of Stephen for that same purpose. Ken rejoined Three's A Crowd in time for their Canadian television debut on CBC's Juliette Show. He toured with them for the remainder of 1966 until another call came from California in early 1967 to join the Buffalo Springfield.

Meanwhile, as Neil and his accomplices journeyed through the American heartland, problems were arising. Neil and Bruce were intensely focused on their mission and friction soon grew between them and their fun-loving companions. "These girls were driving Bruce and I nuts," emphasizes Neil. "They were destroying the car when they would drive and I was paranoid the car was going to break down. I didn't want another Blind River." He was unable to sleep when others drove and would toss about nervously in the back until it was again his turn behind the wheel. Worried over the stamina of the old hearse to endure the lengthy trip, Neil soon took over all the driving duties. It was his vehicle, after all, and only he knew how to treat it, with tenderness and a lighter foot. The physical and mental abuse he put himself through over the hearse, coupled with his anxiety over the ultimate goal of the trip, eventually caught up with him after a few days.

"We got to Albuquerque and I got real sick, almost a nervous breakdown from exhaustion or nerves. I had to lie down for days, three or four days." On a doctor's recommendation, Neil rested. The weary travelers found a friendly place to crash with some college students. There, with Bruce by his side, Neil slept on a mattress on the floor, rising briefly to eat or use the washroom. There was a dark cloud of foreboding among the occupants of the house that perhaps this young Canadian asleep on their floor was seriously ill. However, once Neil had rested sufficiently, the journey was again underway, with a lighter load for this final leg. "We left Tannis, Jeannine, and Mike in Albuquerque and took the long haired red head with us, Bruce and I and this girl heading for L.A." Tannis had found work performing at a coffeehouse near New Mexico State University and the other two opted to stay rather than follow Neil's obsession. "We had passed by this odd looking thing that looked like an igloo in the middle of the desert when we pulled into Albuquerque," recalls Bruce. "It was a coffeehouse called the Igloo. Tannis, of course, being a folksinger, and Jeannine being a close friend, decided to stay and work the club."

Tannis Neiman later returned to Toronto. Sadly, she died a few years ago of cancer. In a touching postscript, Bruce adds, "Neither I nor Neil saw Tannis for years and then one of my tours took me through Toronto and I saw her. Soon after, Neil's tour took him through Toronto and Neil saw her too. Then, two months later she was dead. She willed me her most precious possession," states Bruce, "her Martin twelve string guitar. We hadn't seen each other in over fifteen years and she did that."

It was April first, April Fool's Day, when the hearse, with its trio of frazzled travelers, pulled into Los Angeles. It had been over ten days since they had left Toronto and the initial enthusiasm that had spurred them on at the outset was worn thin. The trip had been much more than any of them had anticipated. It was hardly an auspicious arrival. "We slept in the hearse, parking it on the street at night," relates Neil. "Right away after we got there, the red haired girl got scared, so we sent her home. So it was Bruce and I in L.A." With their mission accomplished, the two set out to find Stephen, unaware of his whereabouts or the fact that Richie was with him. "I knew Stills was down there, but I didn't know where. Bruce didn't know him but I had told him about Stills. I was asking about him in clubs and coffeehouses around L.A." That search strung out into almost a week. "To get money for gas, cigarettes and food, we used to rent out the hearse for rides from a place where there was a scene happening to another scene. But we never heard anything about Stephen, so Bruce and I decided to head north to San Francisco."

What happened next is the stuff of legends. If that meeting between Neil and Stephen in Fort William a year earlier was star-crossed, then their reunion in a Los Angeles traffic jam must have been the result of some divine intervention. Call it karma, destiny, fate, or whatever, but the meeting of Neil Young and Stephen Stills in Los Angeles, a city of millions of people, that day in early April remains one of rock 'n' roll's few truly monumental moments. Neil relates the circumstances. "Bruce and I were just leaving to go to San Francisco. We were on Sunset Boulevard heading north, stopped at a light. The traffic was heavy. Then Stephen and Richie saw us in traffic. Stephen saw this hearse with Ontario licence plates and said, 'I know that guy, it's Neil!'" Stephen and Richie, along with Barry Friedman, pulled up in Barry's van directly behind Neil's hearse. When the light of recognition went on in Stephen's head, he jumped out and ran to the driver's side of the hearse where he banged on the window, startling Neil at first. Once Neil realized who this crazed person was, the two pulled their vehicles into a nearby Ben Franklin store parking lot and everyone exchanged hugs all round, laughing at the quirk of fate which had brought them together again. Stephen told Neil of Barry Friedman's promise to get him work if he could get a group together. Further proof of their desire to include Neil in their new venture came a few hours later when, at Barry's house, Stephen and Richie played and sang their arrangement of *Nowadays Clancy Can't Even Sing.* "They had already learned it and they could sing it great," states Neil. "They were really good singers." Bruce confirms, "We were both aghast at how well they did that song." No further inducements were necessary. Neil and Bruce threw in their lot with Stephen and Richie

"Barry Friedman put us up in the house on Fountain Avenue, got us some equipment, and gave us some money to live," Neil recalls. He immediately went out and purchased another orange Gretsch Chet Atkins model electric guitar. "All we needed was a drummer, then Barry brought Dewey down and we liked him." Dewey Martin, like Neil and Bruce, was born in Canada, Ottawa to be precise, and like the other two, had drifted south in search of fame and fortune. He had worked for a time in Nashville and toured with Faron Young and Roy Orbison before heading west. In

Seattle, Dewey Martin led Sir Walter Raleigh and the Coupons prior to his arrival in Los Angeles and had recently worked with those "bluegrass pickers gone electric," The Dillards. With the lineup now set, the five began rehearsing, working on arrangements of Stephen and Neil's own songs. No cover versions this time, they would do all their own material. In these four young men, Neil had found musicians who shared with him an interest in both folk and rock music and the merger of the two into a unique sound, along with a drive to be successful.

At last, Neil had found musicians whose ideas and goals were congruent with his own. With the combination of songwriting talents, strong singing, and experienced musicianship, the group had what they considered a winning combination. "We were so confident of what we were doing and the sound we had that we saw ourselves as having no competition, other than the Beatles or the Stones," Neil reflects. "It was that good in the beginning." They found to their surprise that they thoroughly enjoyed making music together. Shortly after their rehearsals got underway, the five were sitting on a curb outside the house taking a break when they noticed a steamroller engaged in street resurfacing nearby. The metal name plate on the side read Buffalo-Springfield Roller Co., Toledo, Ohio. The new group had found their name. Neil still possesses that metal name plate today.

A few weeks later, Neil wrote to Rassy back in Winnipeg that he was in Los Angeles and had formed a new group. "The group is called the Buffalo Springfield for no particular reason," he wrote. All that Neil had dreamed of since those early days in Winnipeg, the determination that drove him to leave friends behind in search of his own unique vision, the perseverance he showed through the frustration and rejection in Toronto, was about to pay off.

, drummer	**steve stills,** 2nd lead guitar	**richie furay,** rhythm guitarist	**nell young,** lead guitarist	**bruce palmer,** bass guitarist
	pale blue	easygoing	brown and green	mysterious
	yellow	a true friend	leather and suede	deep
	direct	orange	midnight	zen
	capricorn	taurus	scorpio	beaded moccasins
the group	funloving	open and alert	free	virgo
	youthful—sometimes childlike	miniature golf	deep and dark	purple
	energetic	yellow springs, ohio	winnipeg	the unknown factor
	new orleans	summer breezes	hot and cold	wise
	"steve is the leader,	afternoon	wild sense of humor	safe
	but we all are"		hearses	strong
				inscrutible

Fellow Canadians Dewey Martin and Bruce Palmer teamed up with Neil, Stephen Stills, and Richie Furay to form the Buffalo Springfield.

The back cover of the second Buffalo Spring-field album featured various references to Neil's Canadian friends and influences, including Ken Koblun from The Squires and Ricky James Matthews from The Mynah Birds — and Mort, of course.

Dewey Martin poses with a hockey stick, not drum sticks, in this photo, while Neil wears his buckskin costume.

Neil looks the "other" way on the cover of **Last Time Around.**

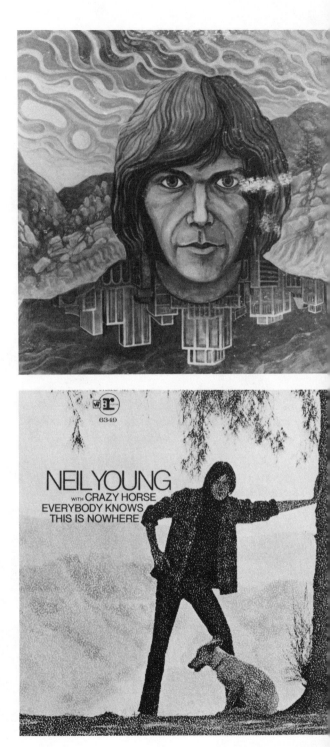

Reproduced here are the cover jackets for Neil's first solo album **Neil Young** *and his first album with* **Crazy Horse,** *featuring the rock anthem* **Down by the River.**

Neil joined David Crosby, Stephen Stills, and Graham Nash for their second album Deja Vu and for their performance at the landmark Woodstock Folk Festival.

ELEVEN

WHEN THE DREAM CAME

*When the dream came, I held my breath
    with my eyes closed
I went insane, like a smoke-ring day
    when the wind blows.
Now I won't be back 'til later on,
If I do come back at all.
But you know me, and I miss you now.*

ON THE WAY HOME, 1968

"It all happened so fast," states Neil on the formation of the Buffalo Springfield in early 1966. "I was down in L.A. and I got this band together with these people who I thought were really good and we were singing our own songs. And all of a sudden things had a different perspective to them. The band was good. People were digging us. I was singing some songs and starting to develop again. It was really good so I just went with it." Neil's years of struggling for an audience in Canada came to an abrupt end within a month of arriving in the United States. Formed immediately after their traffic jam meeting, the Buffalo Springfield were already turning people on to their innovative sound within ten days of coming together. On April 15th, the band debuted on a short seven date tour of Southern California opening for folk rock pioneers, The Byrds. Although financial success was still far off, the young musicians wanted to look every bit the rock stars they would later become. "I used to pick everybody up in the hearse and we would drive it to The Byrds' manager's office," recalls Neil. "Then we would leave it there parked on the street and get into a limousine for the ride to the concert. One day, we got into the hearse and the back end fell out. It needed a U-joint but we couldn't find one so we just left it there."

Despite their warm up status, the Springfield were so impressive that the headliners began showing up early to stand in the wings and watch the young group. The Springfield's hybrid of folk, rock, and country, all presented with an energetic and appealing stage presence, was a winning combination. In an era when the music scene was inclining more towards the guitar virtuoso and extended, self-indulgent jamming was the vogue, the Springfield stepped back, drawing on their collective roots in these varying styles to create a fresh sound that emphasized songwriting and singing.

In June, the band began a six week residency at the legendary Sunset Strip club, the Whiskey A Go Go. The band's musical identity was forged here as was Neil's unique persona. "I would have to say that the six weeks that we were the house band at the Whiskey was probably as dynamic as the band ever was," offers Richie. "It was really something to watch the people line up every night to see us. We played with The Doors there and The Grass Roots but we were the real draw. We really had something in those early months. It's a shame that there's nothing recorded from that time." Dressed in fringed buckskins and suedes, or Comanche war jackets, Neil adopted his Hollywood Indian image. While Stephen and Richie took center stage, Neil was content to stay in the background. "At the start, I was more the guitar player and writer in the band," states Neil, "but that didn't last very long. I started singing my own songs and getting into it again." It was a heady period in Los Angeles with bands like The Byrds, The Mamas and Papas, Love, The Leaves, The Grass Roots, and the early Doors who played the same Sunset Strip clubs as the Springfield, all exploring new sounds and styles. The Springfield's unique sound found fertile ground among both their fans and their peers. Regrettably, the five young musicians were so headstrong and determined to make it that when hurdles came in their path, they couldn't pull together and overcome them as a group.

During their residency at the Whiskey, the band was besieged with recording contracts. "We got the Atlantic-Atco deal from our live gigs at the Whiskey," states Bruce. "We had over twenty offers to sign and we got the whole Hollywood treatment, the guys with the cigars stuffing money in our pockets up in their big offices." The band also signed with influential managers Greene and Stone, whose other clients included Sonny and Cher.

On July 25, the Springfield were once again a warm-up act, but this time it was for the Rolling Stones at the Hollywood Bowl. Although bottom of the bill to the Stones, McCoys, Standells, and Tradewinds, the band managed an impressive four song set that caught the attention of 10,000 screaming fans and the media. For Neil, it been quite a leap from the Hudson Hotel, Churchill to the Hollywood Bowl in a little over one year. And all this without even releasing a record yet!

When the Springfield entered a recording studio, the tensions rose. Both Neil and Stephen wanted their songs on the debut album, knowing the more songs each had, the more royalties each made. Egos began to clash. It would mark the start of a protracted love-hate relationship between the two stubborn musicians. The Springfield's first single was slated to be Stephen's *Go And Say*

Goodbye backed by *Nowadays Clancy Can't Even Sing.* However, under pressure from L.A. radio stations to push *Clancy*, Atco-Atlantic Records complied, flipping the single to make *Clancy* the A side. This move only upped the ante in the feud. Despite an impressive debut chart showing in Los Angeles, *Clancy* stiffed nationally. Middle America was not yet ready for the word "damn" on their AM airwaves. Disheartened but still buoyant with enthusiasm, the band resumed recording their album. When completed, the album featured seven of Stephen's songs and five of Neil's. Of those, Neil only sang lead on two.

Those first recordings reveal five musicians playing as a tight group, the dynamic between them pushing the band to a creative peak early. While Neil's songs remained abstract and deep, Stephen's were straightforward pop songs with an ear to the commercial market. Richie was the man in the middle, holding the two disparate talents together. What seems odd is Neil's reluctance at first to sing lead in Buffalo Springfield. He had persevered through years of slagging over his voice but had always stuck to his guns, only to step back now in the Springfield. On their first album, Richie sings three of Neil's compositions, including *Clancy*. "When I first got there," explains Neil, "Steve and Richie had already worked out *Clancy* with Richie singing it, so it set the precedent." Initially, it was Richie who was perceived as the band's attraction. "We saw Richie as the big strength," states Neil. "He had a strong vocal presence for the band." Richie comments, "Neil didn't have the confidence in his voice. Neil has a very distinct and unique voice and it wasn't until later that he felt more confident about it and people began to accept it more."

In retrospect, the first album would become the only real group effort. It was, from beginning to end, just the five of them making music and digging playing with each other. The two subsequent albums, although brilliant in their diversity and virtuosity, were not albums by a complete group but individuals recording their own songs with the help of a revolving door of sidemen or whichever band member might be around. On the back sleeve of their debut album, a list of words or phrases offered fans an insight into each member. Neil's list included "Winnipeg, Wild Sense of Humor, and Hearses."

Winnipeg had known little of Neil's sudden fame in California. Never one for writing letters, Neil did send a note to his mother and phoned his father to inform them of the group and his excitement over the events that were unfolding that summer. A brief, rather offbeat, note appeared in Jim MacLeod's Modern Music column in the *Winnipeg Tribune* newspaper in early October:

> *The name Neil Young won't attract too much attention when spoken to a passing friend because he won't know who he is. Neil formerly played with The Squires before leaving for California. This young Winnipegger composed songs for that outstanding duet Sonny and Cher.*

It's hard to imagine Sonny and Cher as an outstanding duet, let alone Neil providing songs for them! No mention was made of the Buffalo Springfield or the acclaim they were earning in Los Angeles. Hardly an enthusiastic hometown response.

There was, however, another message coming back to Winnipeg that fall from Neil, and it was much more distressing. Pam Smith, Neil's old Falcon Lake flame, received a lengthy letter followed by a phone call from Neil in L.A. "He wrote me a disturbing letter ten or eleven pages long," Pam recalls. "His thoughts were very disjointed. He said that he was under a lot of pressure from his managers and record company, and the people he hung out with, and he couldn't be himself. He indicated that he was trying drugs." The drug culture was still a few years away from Winnipeg, so this kind of revelation was quite troubling for Pam. "He asked me to write to him every week. He was very busy and he needed some security, something to grab on to because his life was so hectic, in the middle of a storm." His attempt to make contact with Pam comes as no surprise. In an article about the Buffalo Springfield that ran in *TeenSet* in September, Neil was asked, in typical teenybop fashion, to describe his dream girl. His response was, "a combination of summer, Winnipeg, short blond hair, November 11th, Toronto, Falcon Lake, holidays, trees, wind and rain." With the exception of Toronto, these traits fit Pam Smith, whose birthday happens to be one day before Neil's, November 11th. In Neil's troubled mind, Pam and Winnipeg meant a safe haven.

By the fall of 1966, Neil was having difficulty coping with being a member of the band. "I was frustrated," states Neil, "because we didn't do as well as I thought we were going to. Success always seemed evasive. We never got any hits." There were hints of his anxiety in the lyrics to his songs that fall, especially in *Out of My Mind*, recorded on the first Springfield album:

Out of my mind, and I just can't take it anymore.
Left behind, by myself and what I'm living for.
All I hear are screams, from outside the limousines
That are taking me out of my mind.

OUT OF MY MIND, 1966

When the first album was finally released in Winnipeg during January 1967, the hometown showed more enthusiasm. A few more articles on the band appeared in the local "Spins and Needles" column, all referring to "Winnipeg's own Neil Young." Record stores prominently displayed the album. The Hudson's Bay Department Store, home of the popular teen hangout the Paddlewheel Restaurant, filled an entire record rack with the album. Rassy did her bit to promote Neil's band as well. "When the first album arrived, I tore down to CKRC with it for Ron Legge. He put it on right away and nearly went straight up," she laughs. There were various rumors floating about by a few musicians and former friends, each claiming to be the inspiration for *Clancy*. Many were surprised to see Neil credited with playing piano on two songs. Those lessons with Susan Cox and the practice at Smith's and Nentwigs' must have paid off. Neil came home that Christmas to visit Rassy and a few friends. His arrival was low key considering the adulation he was becoming accustomed to in Los Angeles. But he had not returned for attention; it was the comfort and security of home that Neil sought.

During the fall of 1966, Neil had experience his first *grand mal* seizure. Bruce was with him when it happened. "We were in some kind of convention. I think it was a music convention and there was something going on on stage. We were standing in a crowd of hundreds of people and Neil was beside me. Then, all of a sudden, he wasn't. He was on the ground having a seizure. It was pretty frightening." Pressure, frustration, and exhaustion all conspired to bring on this episode of epilepsy.

Soon after, Bruce, too, had his own problems. Busted for possession of marijuana and discovered to be an illegal alien, he was promptly deported back to Canada. All this just as the band's latest single, Stephen's *For What It's Worth*, was climbing the charts. With Bruce out indefinitely, a replacement was needed fast. Neil got in touch with Ken Koblun. On short notice, Ken left Three's A Crowd after an engagement at the Brass Rail club in Halifax, Nova Scotia on January 19 and flew to Los Angeles. There, reunited with Neil, Stephen, and Richie, Ken quickly learned their repertoire and debuted on stage with the Springfield six days later at the Tempo Club in San Francisco. "I thought I was joining the band," offers Ken, "but they thought I was just filling in." Ken stayed with the group until February 10, playing San Bernadino, Santa Barbara, Albuquerque, completing his last gig in Lubbock, Texas. During his brief stint with the Springfield, Ken also performed on the Dick Clark after-school rock showcase, "Where The Action Is," miming to *For What It's Worth*. He never recorded with the band. Dismissing his oldest friend was not easy for Neil. Unable to face him, Neil left Ken a note explaining that he was no longer needed. The news hurt. Ken had always been there for Neil, and he had proven that once again.

In a gesture of reconciliation, Neil later dedicated his six minute musical pastiche, *Broken Arrow*, to Ken on the second Buffalo Springfield album:

Did you see him,
Did you see him?
Did you see him in the river?
He was there to wave to you.
Could you tell that the empty quiver,
Brown skinned Indian,
On the banks that were crowded and narrow,
Held a broken arrow.

BROKEN ARROW, 1967

"Neil dedicated that song to me because it's an Indian term for friendship after a war," explains Ken. "It's not about me. Probably Neil felt guilty for sending me away from the Buffalo Springfield." Neil adds, "I dedicated it to him because he had gone through a rough time." Ken returned to Toronto and resumed gigging, first with singer Elyse Weinberg through the spring, rejoining Three's A Crowd in August, in time to perform with them at Expo 67 in Montreal and to play at recording sessions in October in Los Angeles, but quit the group abruptly in late December 1967. Personal problems plagued Ken for a few years after that, before he returned to Winnipeg and put his life back together.

Nineteen sixty-seven, with all its images of peace, love, and psychedelic colors, was not a good year on a personal level for Neil. Although he did manage to produce some exceptional music, it was the product of inner turmoil and group strife. Throughout that year, Neil was in and out of the band. "It seemed like every two months he'd be gone," recalls Richie. "I think Neil always wanted a solo career and the Buffalo Springfield was his security." The business hassles, tensions within the band, especially between him and Stephen, and his feelings of frustration at not achieving the big break the Springfield so richly deserved, were all just too much for Neil. He left on the eve of their performance on "The Tonight Show" forcing the band to cancel an appearance that would have exposed them to a much wider audience. He also missed the legendary Monterey Pop Festival, The Byrds' David Crosby stepping in to fill the void in the band. One can imagine his sense of distrust when a songwriting royalty for $25,000 due to him for his own compositions was whittled down to a meager $1,000 after all "the guys in the suits" were through. "When I wanted peace and quiet," he told an interviewer later, "I had to consult four other guys."

In retrospect, Neil comments that "the success really didn't come very fast for us. The adulation did, but we really struggled for success and recognition for what we were trying to do and we never really attained it. When people heard the band live, they loved us but that never came across on the records. We never got that sound. Our music wasn't the kind that got accepted across the board. Our contemporaries were groups like The Doors. They were our peers at the time and they cleaned up on us as far as leaving their mark goes and getting hits. We were opening act on most of our shows. We never had the headline status. It really wasn't success. We never really left our mark." Richie offers his assessment of the Springfield's problems: "Everytime we were making a move, there was another guy in the band, so we just couldn't get any consistency. We couldn't sustain the momentum long enough with guys coming and going." He adds, "I don't want to point any fingers, but I think our management didn't really know exactly what to do with us. But to give them the benefit of the doubt, they had some of the same frustrations with the people in and out of the band that we had."

Neil rejoined the group in time for the second album, the critically acclaimed BUFFALO SPRINGFIELD AGAIN, released later that year. The album proved to be the band's high water mark. Although each track revealed the maturity of each of the three songwriters, the album lacked overall cohesiveness, as each song was so different from the others. Unlike the first album, it was difficult for the listener to discern a distinctive Buffalo Springfield sound. The back cover included a thank you list to those people or places that the band members drew influence or inspiration from over the years. Included in the list, and suggested by Neil, were Hank B. Marvin, Randy Bachman, Ian and Sylvia, Ricky James Matthews, Craig Allen (the Allen Ward Trio), Fort William, Mort, and, in large letters, Ken Koblun.

Rassy was able to visit Neil in California and witnessed the band's concert in San Francisco. There, she experienced a Frisco-style psychedelic light show. Later, back in Winnipeg, The Jefferson Airplane played a January concert at the Winnipeg Arena. A light show had been touted as part of their performance, but the band failed to bring one along. Disappointed fans called in to Ron Legge's radio show the next day to air their complaints. Amid the youthful disgruntled harangue came a scratchy, sandpaper-like voice that no one could ignore, from a woman who went on to describe in vivid detail what Winnipeg audiences had missed the night before. She talked of head lights and strobe lights and the impact these had on audiences. When she finished, Ron said, "Thank you Mrs. Young. That was Neil Young's Mom who just came back from seeing Neil's band, the Buffalo Springfield, playing in San Francisco with a light show."

Neil was torn between his love for the band and his need to be on his own, solo and in charge. He could never fully come to terms with being in a band that he wasn't the leader of. Right from those early years in Winnipeg, Neil had called the shots, charted his own course. He would not be happy until he did so. On May 5, 1968, the Buffalo Springfield played their last concert in Long Beach, California. It was a sad end to a band with so much potential. A few months later, their final album, LAST TIME AROUND, was released. Despite the turmoil surrounding the band members who entered the studio separately to record their parts, the album was a fitting conclusion to a talented group. Neil's contributions, *On the Way Home* and *I Am a Child*, were stellar songs and offered insights into his anxieties during that turbulent period. *On the Way Home* chronicles Neil's feelings about the band and his role in and out of it, in an open letter to friend Stephen Stills. It was written during one of Neil's absent periods. Ironically, on the album, it is Richie who sings the song:

> *When the dream came, I held my breath with my eyes closed.*
> *I went insane, like a smoke-ring day when the wind blows.*
> *Now I won't be back 'til later on,*
> *If I do come back at all.*
> *But you know me, and I miss you now.*
>
> *In a strange game, I saw myself as you knew me.*
> *When the change came and you had a chance to see through me.*
> *Though the other side is just the same,*
> *You can tell my dream is real.*
> *But you know me, and I miss you now.*
>
> ON THE WAY HOME, 1968

I Am a Child almost seems like a throw away tune because of its simplicity, yet the lyrics offer much more. Resurrecting part of the chord pattern from *The Rent Is Always Due*, Neil sings of the wide-eyed innocence a child experiences. It is not difficult to connect *I Am a Child* to the theme of *Sugar Mountain*, only here the child is reminding the adult of the joy he feels and brief pleasure he brings during those fleeting early years. Close friends always remember Neil's warmest, yet most private, memories were of those early childhood years in Omemee, Ontario when his family was together:

> *I am a child, I last awhile.*
> *You can't conceive of the pleasure in my smile.*
> *You hold my hand, rough up my hair.*
> *It's lot's of fun to have you there.*
>
> *I gave to you, now you give to me.*
> *I'd like to know what you've learned.*
> *The sky is blue and so is the sea.*
> *What is the color, when black is burned?*
> *What is the color?*
>
> *You are a man, you understand.*
> *You pick me up and you lay me down again.*
> *You make the rules, you say what's fair.*
> *It's lot's of fun to have you there.*

> *I AM A CHILD*, 1968

The cover illustration for LAST TIME AROUND reveals much about the band's troubled legacy. While the other four stand side-by-side, looking ahead, Neil, head turned away, is peering in a different direction. Neil was now free to pursue his own vision once again. He vowed immediately afterward that he would never be a member of a group again. "When we started out," states Neil, "we thought we would be together forever."

TWELVE

JOURNEY THRU THE PAST

When the winter rains come pouring down.
On that new home of mine,
Will you think of me and wonder
    if I'm fine? . . .
Now I'm going back to Canada,
On a journey through the past.
And I won't be back 'til February comes.

Journey Thru The Past, 1973

The summer of 1968 found Neil in a positive, upbeat frame of mind. Signing to Reprise Records and settling down in a house in Topanga Canyon in the Hollywood Hills, Neil experienced a sense of security and comfort for the first time since leaving Winnipeg. The transience and turbulence of the previous four years had taken their toll on him, and although he had yet to achieve financial independence, he was a proven commodity in the music world. He had learned from his experience with the Springfield that having control over his career was essential to his well-being. He could not be satisfied any other way. That summer, Neil began recording his first solo album, simply called NEIL YOUNG, which was released to lukewarm response in January 1969. Around that time, in keeping with his new found independence, Neil embarked on a solo acoustic tour of small clubs. Like his album, reaction to his performances was somewhat indifferent. He did, however, attempt a homecoming, of sorts.

In January 1969, Neil returned to Canada for two important coffeehouse engagements. The choice of these intimate venues suited his current approach, back to a simpler, acoustic folk style. On January 28th, he appeared at Le Hibou in Ottawa for a one week stand. The following week, Neil made his return to Toronto at the prestigious Riverboat coffeehouse in Yorkville. Just three years earlier, he couldn't beg a gig at that club. Now here he was, alone on the small stage, his peers, contemporaries, and former critics all present to witness Neil Young's uniquely personal vision. In many ways, that vision had changed little from the time he was scuffling for attention in Yorkville. Yet now he was a little more worldly and wise both to the music business and to himself. The collective inferiority complex of Canadians, which forces its own to achieve recognition elsewhere before receiving it at home, was in full evidence that week. California had embraced him, so now it was okay for Canada to do the same. Neither gig was an overwhelming success, but Neil had served notice that he was a major talent and, very soon, would prove that point beyond Canada's wildest expectations.

A reviewer in Ottawa cited Neil's Springfield tunes as the highlight of his set, noting that the newer material had a sameness to it, not unlike Bob Dylan's earlier acoustic folk work. He concluded that "there's a lot of poetry in his music, and a lot of wit." The lyrics from several songs of the NEIL YOUNG album are also distinctively poetic. Perhaps the song *The Loner* is most memorable and telling:

> *he's a perfect stranger like a cross of himself and a fox. he's a feeling arranger and a changer of the way he talks. he's the unforeseen danger, the keeper of the key to the locks. if you see him on the subway he'll be down at the end of the car watching you move until he knows who you are. when you get off your station alone he'll know that you are. there was a woman he knew about a year or so ago. she had something that he needed and he pleaded with her not to go. on the day that she left he died but it did not show. know when you see him nothing can free him. step aside. open wide. its the loner.*

THE LONER, 1968

The Toronto engagement proved to be Neil's reconciliation with Yorkville. Even his father attended one of the Riverboat performances, seeing his son for the first time as a musician. He immediately became a Neil Young fan. Reviews in *The Globe and Mail*, his father's employer, and the *Toronto Daily Star* were favorable. Jack Batten, writing in the *Daily Star*, couldn't help but notice a Canadian presence to Neil's songs and performance, comparing his voice to that of another former Torontonian, Rick Danko of The Band. To *The Globe*'s Ritchie Yorke, Neil offered this revelation: "I want to come back to live in Canada soon. I'm trying to get an artist's visa, which allows you to move around from country to country. As soon as I can get it, I'll move back."

No such move took place. Back in California, Neil's career would accelerate so quickly that year he would have little time to think about residency in Canada. In rapid succession, Neil formed a new backing group, Crazy Horse, released a well-received album entitled EVERYBODY KNOWS THIS IS NOWHERE, and joined the already acclaimed "supergroup" (a term coined to describe this new phenomenon) Crosby, Stills, and Nash, adding "& Young" to their masthead. Certainly, one could argue, Neil was once again jumping headfirst into the band situation, contradicting his previous edicts after the demise of the Springfield. In reality, Neil was merely accepting limited partnerships in both aggregations. The relationships he established with both groups were loose, allowing him the freedom to work with either, or none, maintaining his burgeoning solo identity. Even the decision to call a band by the name of its individuals, like a law firm or business partnership, rather than a collective identity was a radical departure. Neil's arrangement was unusual to a rock world brought up to expect a sense of commitment in its bands. Through thick and thin, the Beatles were still a foursome, at least in the eyes of the public who knew little of the bickering behind the scenes. Despite the death of Brian Jones that year, the Rolling Stones remained a unit. Now, here was Neil Young, hardly a household name or bankable artist in his own right, shaking up the traditional group dynamic by having it three different ways. He now had the freedom to pursue his musical vision anyway he chose. "I'm the boss," he told journalist Ritchie Yorke. "I wouldn't work as a member of a group again. At first I felt guilty. Then I realized that's where I'm at." For those who knew Neil, it was not an expression of ego, but reality. He had spent too long in control of his own destiny to lose it now that success was just down the road.

In August 1969, Neil, in the company of Crosby, Stills, and Nash, appeared at the legendary Woodstock Festival. Years later, commenting to Jack Harper about the path his career had taken since leaving Winnipeg, Neil remarked that in the space of four short years he had gone from River Heights Community Club to Woodstock, a progression that spanned much more than merely miles or years. By 1969, Neil found himself, rather surprisingly, a part of what rock music analysts and insiders dubbed the next big thing in music, the Canadian Invasion. Canadian artists like The Guess Who, Anne Murray, Andy Kim, The Poppy Family, Motherlode, The Five Man Electrical Band, and The Original Caste were dominating the American singles and album record charts. Neil, along with Joni Mitchell, Leonard Cohen, and The Band, had become the darlings of the post-hippie, FM music set, despite the fact that each of them had been operating out of the United States for years and had, in fact, been forced by indifference at home to flee southward to find success. Nonetheless, they all held Canadian birth certificates, the only prerequisite it seemed for membership in this much ballyhooed trend. Patriotism ran rampant as Canadian rock journalists fell over themselves exhalting the praises of homeground talent. Suddenly, being Canadian was cool. The Guess Who appeared on stage each night across the U.S.A. with a huge Canadian flag as their backdrop and a smiling beaver for their logo. What was unique about this brief explosion of Canadian music on the international scene was that most of these artists had found success across the border without having to abandon their homeland. The times had indeed changed for Canadian artists since Neil, Joni, and many others had fled. Unlike the British Invasion, the Canadian counterpart was only a shortlived warm breeze from the north and had a minimal impact on the overall music scene. Neil's momentum was not affected by his association with this brief flash.

With the release in 1970 of both a CSN&Y album, DEJA VU, and another Neil Young solo album, AFTER THE GOLDRUSH, Neil's star was indeed rising to superstar levels. Drawing on his childhood memories once again for inspiration, Neil wrote *Helpless*, recording it with Crosby, Stills, Nash & Young for their DEJA VU album. The song finds Neil in a melancholy mood, describing important childhood images of his years in Omemee he had stored away for so long. Yet he recognizes that he cannot go back to those days; the door to that period, when he was happiest and his mother and father were still together, are firmly shut behind him:

> *There is a town in North Ontario,*
> *With dream comfort memory to spare.*
> *And in my mind, I still need a place to go,*
> *All my changes were there.*
> *Blue, blue windows behind the stars,*
> *Yellow moon on the rise.*
> *Big birds flying across the sky,*
> *Throwing shadows on our eyes.*

Leave us helpless, helpless, helpless.
The chains are locked and tied across the door.
Baby sing it with me somehow.

HELPLESS, 1970

The song, an acknowledgement of Neil's Canadian roots, has endured as a concert favorite for years. Appropriately, Neil chose to perform *Helpless* along with Ian Tyson's *Four Strong Winds* at The Band's 1976 farewell concert, The Last Waltz, accompanied by Joni Mitchell and The Band members themselves, whose roots are also firmly planted in rural Ontario. They were all young Canadians, away from home, cherishing those memories.

DEJA VU and AFTER THE GOLDRUSH sold in the millions and the cash flow to Neil was staggering. Grabbing what he could before taxes nabbed the bulk of it, Neil purchased Broken Arrow Ranch, located near San Francisco. When Neil first looked over his property, the old ranch hand who worked there, Louis Avila (the inspiration for his song, *Old Man* on his HARVEST album), asked him how a young man could have the money to buy such a large estate. Neil replied, "I'm just lucky, I guess." Retreating to get the ranch into shape that fall, Neil was home amid the redwoods and rolling hills. It is still his home, his longest permanent residence ever. The serenity of the ranch, coupled with the enormous amount of praise heaped upon him that year, caused Neil to pause for reflection. The result of that break would be his solo acoustic "Journey Thru The Past" tour that would take him across Canada for the first time.

Prior to the Canadian leg of the tour, Neil had made his triumphant debut at Carnegie Hall, performing two shows. His mother attended one, his father the other. A recent back injury incurred while moving timber beams on the ranch had put Neil in a back brace for the all-important Canadian portion of the tour after Christmas. Commencing in Vancouver on January 6, 1971, Neil made his way to the concert halls of various major Canadian cities with a few detours into the northern U.S. Reviews were unanimously positive at each stop. Each critic seemed to find it somehow necessary to attach some kind of Canadian chauvinism to Neil Young. Jack Batten went on again about the "peculiarly Canadian touch in his voice, a light, fresh, high sound that suggests wide, clear, open land." Perhaps, too, it may have been his stage garb for the tour — checkered, flannel lumberjack shirt, tails hanging out, heavy, laced-up work boots, tattered, patched jeans, at some shows even a toque. He was the Great White North come to life. It was as if Neil had just been out chopping some fire wood on the ranch and, wandering into the log house, discovered a few thousand people waiting for a song.

On Wednesday evening, January 13, Neil Young made his return to Winnipeg. It had been six years since he last graced a stage there, and many old friends and fans came out to welcome him home. He had left Winnipeg years earlier as a rock 'n' roller with a dream; now he had returned as rock's premier singer/songwriter. It had been quite a journey. With barely any advertising, ticket demand at the Centennial Concert Hall was so great that two shows were scheduled that evening. The word was out that Neil was back. Everyone entering the hall was checked for cameras and tape recorders. Neil did not like to be distracted by camera flashes, concertgoers were informed as they shuffled through the turnstiles. Appearing alone on the stark stage with just acoustic guitar and piano, lumberjack outfit and back brace that kept him stiffly in a wooden-backed chair, Neil proceeded to mesmerize the capacity crowd. Bent over his acoustic guitar, head down, eyes closed, long, straight hair draping past his shoulders, Neil spoke rarely, choosing, like he always had, to let his music speak for him. The odd reference was made to being home and to people in the crowd. "There's a guy out there in the audience who used to tune my guitar," he offered. The intensity of his performance led those in the audience to feel that they were in the presence, not of a local boy-made-good, but a world-class singer/songwriter. It was a magical night.

Walking onstage without introduction and offering no greetings, Neil opened the show with the Buffalo Springfield's *On The Way Home*. It seemed a fitting number for the tour. Throughout the concert, Neil interspersed the familiar with new material, much of it written recently on his ranch. Some, like *Heart of Gold*, *Old Man*, and *A Man Needs a Maid*, appeared a year later on his

HARVEST album. Others, like *See the Sky About To Rain, Dance, Dance, Dance,* and *Bad Fog of Loneliness* would wait much longer to appear on vinyl. For the Winnipeg show, Neil added *Clancy* to his set, to unrestrained applause.

Afterwards, Neil hosted a party for family and friends at the posh, downtown Winnipeg Inn. The general theme of the conversations floating about the room focused on how each individual present just knew that Neil would make it someday. Neil mingled among the patrons, hugging, shaking hands and reminiscing. As is the case with these post-concert soirées, the room was well represented by hangers-on, the radio and record company set, most of whom didn't know Neil's name from Adam two years earlier. Neil was disappointed that many of the former Squires were not present. In particular, he had wanted to see Allan Bates and Ken Smyth. "I was looking for them but I didn't find them," recalls Neil. "You never realize at the time that you'll never see people again." Asked years later about his absence that night, Ken replies, "We weren't sure if he would remember us." Pam Smith adds, "I was afraid that my life would seem so trivial compared to who he was now and all the things he had done. He was somebody and we were all still just here."

Neil spent some time the next day visiting a few old haunts and meeting relatives still in the city. Rassy had since left Winnipeg for New Smyrna Beach, Florida, but Neil still had his Aunt Vinia and Uncle Neil as well as other family friends in Winnipeg. The hectic pace of the tour forced Neil to move on, but his brief stop in his old hometown had been a personal triumph and a kind of reconciliation with his past.

The Journey Thru The Past tour would bring Neil to Massey Hall, Toronto's premier concert venue, a few days later for another triumphant homecoming and for another significant reconciliation with his father. During the Massey Hall concert, Neil acknowledged his father's presence in the audience. He also sang *Old Man*, which Scott Young heard as a note of reconciliation:

Old man take a look at my life. I'm a lot like you were.
Old man look at my life — twenty-four and there's so much more.
Live alone in a paradise that makes me think of two.

Love lost, such a cost, give me things that don't get lost.
Like a coin that won't get tossed
Rolling home to you.

OLD MAN, 1971

Backstage, Scott hailed Neil through the crowd with the words, "Different from the last time." Neil replied, enthusiastically, "Sure is!"

Although Toronto, Vancouver, and Montreal became regular stops on Neil's North American tours throughout the 1970s and early 1980s, it would be thirteen years before he appeared in Winnipeg again. This time it was during his country music phase with his band The International Harvesters. It was a brief stop on his tour itinerary and offered little time for reminiscing. He did, however, manage to assemble much of his family for the gig, with Scott and Neil's grandmother Jean Young from Flin Flon in attendance.

The events which brought him home again were the Shakin' All Over Sixties Winnipeg Bands Reunion and his high school reunion, Kelvin High's 75th anniversary, both held on the weekend of June 28, 1987. Neil had just returned from a European tour with Crazy Horse and was ready for a rest. The trip to Winnipeg offered that and more.

Neil and his wife Pegi had arrived in Winnipeg Saturday morning. Their plan was to attend both reunion events and see as many old friends as possible. On Saturday afternoon, as Neil strolled into the Paddlewheel Restaurant, the "in" hang out in the 1960s, on the sixth floor of the downtown Hudson's Bay Department Store, he called out to the assembled musicians, "Where's Bates and Smyth? Where's The Squires? I want to see my old band!" As Neil made his way through the swarm of fans, he found the two friends he had been looking for, along with Ken Koblun, Terry Crosby, and Jack Harper. Hugging each one, Neil then found a quiet backroom and convened a Squires' reunion. They had a lot of catching up to do, he told a throng of reporters. Posing for a photograph together, Allan Bates remarked at the paths each had followed. Here they all were, middle-aged, successful in their chosen vocations. Neil was in impressive company. Two had earned

Ph.D.'s, one was a bank manager, another an owner of a successful engineering firm, and one a computer programmer. And there was Neil, still playing rock 'n' roll!

That afternoon, Neil and Jack had driven through Crescent-wood, Neil's old neighborhood in south Winnipeg, past the house at 1123 Grosvenor where Neil and his mom had lived, past River Heights and Crescentwood Community Clubs where Neil's early bands had performed. "There are so many memories swirling around in my head," he told Jack. As the two pulled up to Kelvin High School for the reunion, the school wasn't the same as Neil remembered it. The old building, the one he and Jack had attend-ed, had been demolished in the late 1960s to make way for a mod-ern new school. Inside, Neil was once again plagued by crowds. A few among the crowd had been classmates, but many more who pushed their way towards him had paid him scant attention back in their school days. Now that he was a success, everybody claimed to be his best friend. No matter, Neil, ever gracious, smiled and said hello to all of them. Neil was the star attraction for the Kelvin alumni reunion, odd considering that he dropped out after failing grade eleven. In the evening Neil, Jack, and their wives attended the Kelvin dinner. Everyone was dressed in tuxe-dos and evening gowns. Neil, always the rebel, wore his leather jacket. Later that same evening, Neil relived his past when The Squires regrouped on stage at the Blue Note Cafe. For Neil, that evening was the real highlight of the weekend.

At the Shakin' All Over reunion concert on Sunday evening at the Winnipeg Convention Center, four thousand people had come to relive their own past with the bands who had been so important to them. Neil reminisced backstage with his old con-temporaries, those bands and musicians who had all competed with one another for the community club gigs throughout the city. The Galaxies were there, and The Shondels, as well as Carmine LaRosa and the Thunderstorms. Neil shared stories with Burton Cummings who, as leader of The Guess Who, had achieved success in the early 1970s. Burton had led The Deverons, rivals of The Squires. Neil also talked with his former idol, guitarist Randy Bachman. Randy had been the city's first guitar hero and Neil had been a devoted disciple. Randy had earned success first with The

Guess Who and later with Bachman-Turner Overdrive. The two guitarists talked of a possible jam session later. Doc Steen and Ron Legge came by to shake Neil's hand. Both had been DJ's at CKRC radio and had been important boosters of his early career. Everywhere he turned, Neil found old friends and warm memories. Later, Neil was called on stage to receive the Order of the Buffalo Hunt, the highest honor bestowed on a Manitoban, by the provincial government's Minister of Culture. He then approached the microphone and, attempting to calm the crowd, gave a short speech recognizing the pioneering talent of local record producer Harry Taylor. "This guy got us all started making records. I was one of his first experiments. He went on to record all the other groups in town. He just had makeshift equipment down at CKRC and everybody was nervous about making records. This is the guy with the Winnipeg sound, Mr. Harry Taylor."

Following the last band, Neil, Randy Bachman, and Burton Cummings took to the stage to lead the backing band through a jam that included The Guess Who's *American Woman*, Neil's *Down by the River*, Bob Dylan's *Just Like Tom Thumb's Blues*, and closed with a rousing version of Randy's *Takin' Care of Business*. "Jamming with Neil was like going to heaven!" stated Randy after the show. "Honestly, it's one of the highlights of my life. He and I had never played together, so it was an affectionate, joyous occasion for me. Back then I admired his spirit and his determination. We'd all had the same high-school dream — to play rock 'n' roll." As they left the stage amid the roar from the crowd, the three hugged and shouted, "Thank you Winnipeg! This is our home and always will be!" The kid with the dream of a life in music, who believed in himself when few others did, and who had the determination to pursue his goal to the end, had finally come home.

In October 1984, Neil returned to Winnipeg with his band The International Harvesters to perform at the Winnipeg Arena. His wife Pegi accompanied him on this tour.

At the Shakin' All Over concert, Neil jammed with his guitar mentor Randy Bachman, playing Young's Down by the River *and Bachman's* Takin' Care of Business.

Variety Club of Manitoba & Coca-Cola Classic presents

THE Event of 1987

Shakin' All Over

SPECIAL APPEARANCES
by Neil Young, Burton Cummings & Randy Bachman

Do you remember ... This is a once in a lifetime opportunity to hear: Chad Allan, the Quid, the Mongrels, the Jury, the Shondels, the Pallbearers, the Vaqueros, the Club 63 Galaxies, Carmine LaRosa and the Thunderstorms, and Wayne Walker and the Strollers. Join the MC's Doc Steen, Boyd Kozak, Pat Riordan, Bob Burns, and MacLean and MacLean and special guests.

Sunday, June 28, 1987 • 5 pm - 10 pm
3rd Floor, Convention Centre • $19.60 plus service fee

Sponsored by Coca-Cola   **Tickets available at Select-A-Seat**

At this reunion concert, Winnipeg rock legends received the Order of the Buffalo Hunt from the provincial government of Manitoba. Left to right — Burton Cummings, Chad Allan, Neil Young, Randy Bachman, Fred Turner.

ACKNOWLEDGEMENTS

Sections of this book have appeared in various early stages of research and development in *Broken Arrow, Goldmine, Mid Continental*, and in the NYAS booklet *Aurora: The Story of Neil Young and The Squires*.

I would like to extend my thanks to all those people who agreed to share their memories with me and whose names appear throughout this book. In addition, I would like to thank the following for their assistance and advice: Joel Bernstein; Alan Jenkins of the Neil Young Appreciation Society (2A Llynfi Street, Bridgend, Mid Glamorgan, Wales, UK); Pete Long (Neil Young archivist extraordinaire, London, England); Roland Kron (Sonnentanz-Druck +Verlag, Augsburg Germany); Bob Hilderley (Quarry Press, Kingston, Ontario); Debbie Kuypers; David Wittman and Judith Wittman; Susan Irving; Shirley Lord; Sid Rogers; Marilyne White; Jacolyne Harvey; Pam Heintz; Richard Dubord; Tom Horricks; Jay Telfer; Bob Johnson (CKY-TV, Winnipeg); *The Winnipeg Free Press* archives; Gary Yan; Geordie McDonald; Richie Furay (for the positive vibes and photograph); Ray (Dee) Delatinsky (for keeping those tapes all those years); the Get Backs — Glenn MacRae, Bonnie Wallace, Jim Maxwell, Ron Adams, and Captain Jim Drysdale (for all the good times); Thora Cook (Western Canada Pictorial Index, University of Winnipeg); Carey Lauder (for extra-special photography); Miss Jenni Irving (for convincing her Mom to talk to me); David Timms (for the use of his tape recorder); Marc Coulavin (Canadian Music Network); Douglas MacKay (Editor-in-Chief, the *Halifax Daily News*); *Vox Magazine* (for their encouraging review of *Aurora*); Mrs. Edith Banman (for all those courier parcels and phone messages); and my students at St. John's-Ravenscourt School (who, besides being the best students anyone could ever teach, now know more about Neil Young than any other students in the country).

Special thanks to Ken Koblun, The Squires official archivist and original Squire from beginning to end. Thanks, Neil, for your time and cooperation.

I would like to extend a very special thank you to my wife Harriett, for her invaluable editing advice, patience, and tireless support. Also, thanks to Don and Helen Einarson, my Mom and Dad, for their generous support throughout this project. And thanks to my children, Matt and Lynsey, who were once again willing to give me the time to work. This book is dedicated to you, Matt and Lynsey.

CREDITS

COVER

Front cover art by Tom Kapas, from a photograph by William Coupon, reproduced by permission of the artist and the photographer. Back cover photograph of Neil Young performing at Massey Hall from the Horst Ebricht Collection, National Archives of Canada.

PHOTOGRAPHS

Unless otherwise credited here, all photographs, clippings, memorabilia, and album jackets reproduced in this book are from the collection of John Einarson:

p. 9:	Carey Lauder
p. 10 top:	Dan Neil
p. 10 bottom:	Terry Crosby
p. 11 top:	Variety Club of Manitoba
p. 35 top:	Sid Rogers
p. 36 top:	Bob Johnson, CKY-TV Promotions, Winnipeg Free Press, Western Canada Pictorial Index
p. 38:	Shirley Lord
p. 39 top:	Western Canada Pictorial Index
p. 40 top:	Shirley Lord
p. 40 middle:	Shirley Lord
p. 40 bottom:	Richard Dubord
p. 41 top:	Colin Palmer
p. 78 top left:	Ron Simenik
p. 80 bottom right:	Mrs. Liz Clark and Jack Harper
p. 111 top:	Mrs. Liz Clark
p. 112 top:	Scott Shields and Tom Horricks
p. 113:	Mrs. Liz Clark

p. 148:	Canadian Press Files
p. 149:	Jay Telfer
p. 150-51:	Horst Ebricht Collection, National Archives of Canada
p. 152:	Canadian Press Files
p. 187 top:	Richie Furay Collection
p. 189 top:	Canadian Press Files
p. 215 top:	Ken Gigliotti, Winnipeg Free Press, Western Canada Pictorial Index
p. 215 bottom:	Wayne Glowacki, Winnipeg Free Press, Western Canada Pictorial Index
p. 216:	Carey Lauder
p. 217:	Variety Club of Manitoba

LYRICS

Lyrics from various Neil Young songs appear in this book under copyright by the following publishers:

Cotillion/Broken Arrow Music: *Sugar Mountain; Here We Are in the Years; The Last Trip to Tulsa; The Loner; Helpless.*

Springalo-Cotillion Music: *On the Way Home; I Am a Child.*

Broken Arrow Music: *Old Man.*

Ten East, Springalo, Cotillion Music: *Nowadays Clancy Can't Even Sing ; Out of My Mind; Broken Arrow.*

Silver Fiddle Music: *Long May You Run; Don't Be Denied; Ambulance Blues; Don't Pity Me Babe; Journey Thru the Past; Prisoners of Rock 'n' Roll; Country Home.*

Lyrics from *I Wonder* and *Be My Girl* are provided courtesy of Jacolyne Harvey and Marilyne White.

Lyrics from *Hello Lonely Woman, The Rent Is Always Due, Extra, Extra,* and *Sweet Joni* appear courtesy of *Broken Arrow: Neil Young Appreciation Society.*